'This necessary reclaiming of the female narrative in the resistance to apartheid unmutes the voices of many extraordinary, long-suffering women.'
– **Margaret Busby,** *CBE, Hon. FRSL*

'A vivid, moving and gripping book. Focussing with great empathy on the experiences in solitary confinement of four women, Naidoo brings to life the female experience of apartheid. Through these deeply personal stories, she explores the role played by trauma in shaping people's lives. This unique book is a must read.'
– **Mary Harper,** *BBC Africa Editor*

'This book does the tangible work of elevating the many untold stories and lives of women in the struggle for democracy in South Africa. As one turns the pages, you are left stirred with visceral emotions because we are these women, and they are us. This work is important in the collective healing of the wounds in our hearts.'
– **Dr Tlaleng Mofokeng,**
UNHCR Rapporteur on the right to health

'In this unique book, Shanthini Naidoo offers new ways of understanding the ongoing trauma experienced by individuals, communities and nation states following political oppression and armed conflict. Focused on the stories of four female South African freedom fighters, the frequently unknown or unacknowledged female struggle against apartheid is centered and celebrated. Critically, the importance of listening, telling and understanding, as a way of achieving justice and freedom, is laid out.

Beautifully written, *Women in Solitary* is both a powerful and accessible contribution to life-story research, providing insights into the importance of storytelling as an act of remembrance and healing. These extraordinary stories tell us about the gendered experience of resistance, as well as the indelible connections between state institutions and individual actors. In doing so, this book will be of great interest to scholars across the social sciences and humanities.'
– **Dr Finola Farrant,** *Head of Department Social Sciences,*
University of Roehampton, UK

'In this important and so eloquently written book, Shanthini Naidoo narrates the stories of women who shaped South Africa's political life. Their lived experiences of trauma, torture, and imprisonment craft a critical lens through which to examine the complex struggles of women activists. This is thought-provoking reading that will interest organisers, campaigners and scholars alike. It has much to offer to both the untold herstories of South Africa, as well as broader debates in gender studies and critical criminal justice scholarship.'
– **Dr Anastasia Chamberlen,**
University of Warwick, UK

Women in Solitary

Women in Solitary offers a new account based around the narratives of four women who experienced detention and torture in South Africa in the late 1960s when the regime tried to stage a trial to convict leading anti-apartheid activists.

This timely book not only accords the four women and others their place in the history of the struggle for freedom in South Africa, but also weaves their experiences into the historical development of the anti-apartheid movement. The book draws on extended interviews with journalist Joyce Sikhakhane-Rankin, trade unionists Shanthie Naidoo and Rita Ndzanga and activist Nondwe Mankahla. Winnie Mandela's account of her time in detention is drawn from earlier published accounts. The narrative brings to light the unrelentingly brutal and comprehensive character of the attempt to silence resistance and break the spirit of the activists, both to disrupt organisation and to intimidate communities. It is testament to the triumph and strength of conviction that the women displayed. It also reflects the comprehensive nature of the resistance. The women fought not only as organisers, recruiters or couriers, but also in solitary confinement, resisting all its deprivations, the taunts by interrogators and anxieties about their children. And when they took the fight into the courtroom, they prevailed. The book weaves their experiences into the historical development of the struggle in a way that highlights broader issues, drawing out the particular ways in which women's experience of activism and repression differs from that of men, in terms both of the behaviour of the police and of the women's ties with community, family and children.

The book's broad timespan underpins the psychological effects of sustained solitary confinement and its traumatic legacy, asking whether, by not attending more consistently to healing the trauma done to a generation by brutal repression, we allow it to contribute to social ills that worry us today. *Women in Solitary* is ideal reading for anyone interested in the history of apartheid, the criminalisation of activism and women's imprisonment, as well as scholars and students of penal and feminist studies.

Shanthini Naidoo is a former *Sunday Times* (South Africa) journalist who works in content marketing. She has also worked for *The Times* newspaper and *O, The Oprah Magazine*. Naidoo lives in Johannesburg and holds a Master's degree in Journalism and Media Studies from the University of the Witwatersrand. The thesis "Women in Solitary" forms the basis of this book.

Women in Solitary
Inside South Africa's Female Resistance to Apartheid

Shanthini Naidoo

Routledge
Taylor & Francis Group

LONDON AND NEW YORK

Cover by Polygram

First published 2022
by Routledge
2 Park Square, Milton Park, Abingdon, Oxon OX14 4RN

and by Routledge
605 Third Avenue, New York, NY 10158

Routledge is an imprint of the Taylor & Francis Group, an informa business

© 2022 Shanthini Naidoo

(Originally Published by Tafelberg, an imprint of NB Publishers, Cape Town, South Africa in 2020)

The right of Shanthini Naidoo to be identified as author of this work has been asserted by her in accordance with sections 77 and 78 of the Copyright, Designs and Patents Act 1988.

British Library Cataloguing-in-Publication Data
A catalogue record for this book is available from the British Library

Library of Congress Cataloging-in-Publication Data
Names: Naidoo, Shanthini, author.
Title: Women in solitary: inside South Africa's female
resistance to apartheid / Shanthini Naidoo.
Description: Milton Park, Abingdon, Oxon; New York,
NY: Routledge, 2022. | Includes bibliographical references and index. |
Identifiers: LCCN 2021030154 (print) | LCCN 2021030155 (ebook) |
ISBN 9781032133676 (hardback) | ISBN 9781032133652 (paperback) |
ISBN 9781003228905 (ebook)
Subjects: LCSH: Women political prisoners—South Africa. |
Women anti-apartheid activists—South Africa. | Solitary
confinement—South Africa. | South Africa—Politics and
government—20th century.
Classification: LCC HV9850.5 .N35 2022 (print) |
LCC HV9850.5 (ebook) | DDC 365/.450820968—dc23
LC record available at https://lccn.loc.gov/2021030154
LC ebook record available at https://lccn.loc.gov/2021030155

ISBN: 978-1-032-13367-6 (hbk)
ISBN: 978-1-032-13365-2 (pbk)
ISBN: 978-1-003-22890-5 (ebk)

DOI: 10.4324/9781003228905

Typeset in Times New Roman
by codeMantra

For Veradya and Yovari
May you always find your strength

Contents

Acknowledgements

To the women in this story and their families. You shared your lives with me, and I will always be grateful. It has been a joy getting to know you. Shanthie Naidoo and Dominic Tweedie, especially Dominic's history lessons. Joyce Sikhakhane-Rankin, and her children, Samora, Oliver, Vikela, Nomzamo and Allan. Nondwe Mankahla and her daughter, Phila. Ma Rita Ndzanga, Cecil and Laurette.

Lesley Cowling, for instigating this book by supervising my Wits journey.

My publishers, Gill Moodie, Helena Cobban and Lydia de Cruz and Editorial Assistant Arunima Aditya for your contribution to getting this book out into the world.

Prof Pumla Gobodo-Madikizela, Dr Tlaleng Mofokeng, Ferial Haffajee and Michele Magwood. It was an honour to have you read the first drafts. Donna Bryson, Dr Barbara Ransby, Dr Gwendolyn Zoharah Simmons and the many reviewers.

The Ahmed Kathrada Foundation. The Nelson Mandela Foundation. W.W. Norton & Company, New York.

The Khulumani Support Group.

The University of the Witwatersrand, for the historical papers and Shirona Patel for your assistance.

The SABC TRC transcripts.

The Apartheid Museum.

For the recent photos: Alaister Russell, Fredlin Adriaan, Alon Skuy, Phil Makagoe.

My *Sunday Times* editors, Nadine Dreyer, Sue de Groot, and colleagues Peta Scop and Keith Taamkei for the early days.

Leizl Eykelhof for edits. Best friend and first eye, Charl Amin, who knew I could do this before I did. Winston Mangaru for the laughs. My dearest Lihle Z Mtshali, Karen van Rooyen, Qaanitah Hunter and Laura Lopez Gonzalez.

My husband, Mervin Chetty, and my girls for the stolen time. I've made it up to you.

Linah Moyo for all your help.

My family, especially my sisters, Shivani and Divasha, and my brother, Huday, for your support.

My mother, Pat Naidoo, and my grandmother, Valliamma Naicker, for being the first strong women I knew. My late dad, Krish Naidoo, for instilling the love of learning.

About the author

Shanthini Naidoo is a former *Sunday Times* journalist who works in content marketing. She has also worked for *The Times* daily newspaper and *O, The Oprah Magazine*. Naidoo lives in Johannesburg with her husband and two daughters.

Glossary

1954 Bantu Education Act: one of a series of acts following the 1948 whites-only election that brought the National Party to power; it downgraded the education available to blacks (Bantu), in apartheid terminology.

1956 Treason Trial: trial on charges of treason of 156 imprisoned leaders of the 1955 Congress of the People (see below); the trial lasted five years but all defendants were eventually acquitted.

Ahmed Kathrada Foundation: foundation named for a man convicted and imprisoned alongside Mandela; it archives material related to South Africa's freedom struggle.

Amandla salute: "Amandla!" means "power!" and is part of the slogan "Amandla Awethu!" – power to the people. Earlier, the salute was a closed fist with a raised thumb but now it is usually a raised, clenched fist.

ANC: African National Congress, a national liberation movement founded in 1912. The ANC expanded fast in the 1950s and was banned in 1960 but it continued to organise in exile and clandestinely within South Africa and won the first universal-franchise elections in 1994 with a large majority.

apartheid: apartness or segregation (in Afrikaans, the majority language among "Whites" in South Africa); from 1948 through 1994 segregation by race, and privilege for "Whites," was law in South Africa.

AWO: Alexandra Women's Organisation, a grouping in Alexandra, a Black "township," near Johannesburg. A "township" or "location" was a place where the laws of the apartheid era allowed designated types of non-"White" people to live.

bakkie: a pick-up truck.

bashile amabantwana: colloquialism that translates literally as "the children were burned."

Black Consciousness Movement: movement that grew up during the exile of the ANC, many of whose members later joined the ANC; its most famous exponent was the martyr Steve Biko.

Black Sash: organisation of "White" South African women who opposed apartheid through non-violent actions; it was founded in 1955 and did courageous work from then until after the official end of apartheid.

BOSS: Bureau of State Security, South Africa's senior intelligence service 1969–80; it reported directly to the Prime Minister.

braai: barbecue, meat cooked over charcoal (Afrikaans).

Buti: brother.

Buti Nel: Brother Nelson (Mandela).

Congress of the People; Freedom Charter: the Congress was a June 1955 gathering of delegates from all over South Africa, preceded by nation-wide consultations; it adopted the Freedom Charter, which declared that "South Africa belongs to all who live in it, black and white." Five organisations signed the Charter, the largest being the ANC.

COSATU: Congress of South African Trade Unions, South Africa's largest labour union federation, allied to the ANC. (Dominic Tweedie was not "secretary" of COSATU, but worked in its Communications Department.)

Defiance Campaign: a campaign the ANC launched in 1952 to protest unjust laws like the 1950 Suppression of Communism Act, 1950, the 1952 Pass Laws Act, etc.

dompas: passbook (ID document) that all Blacks were forced to carry; police arrested and locked people up daily, in the thousands, for not carrying a passbook, or for being in the wrong place according to the passbook.

FEDSAW: Federation of South African Women, a non-racial national women's organisation launched in 1954 with the release of an anti-apartheid declaration called the Women's Charter. On 9 August 1956, it organised a famous march to the Union Buildings (the seat of government) in Pretoria to protest the extension of the pass laws to women; 9 August is now Women's Day in South Africa.

FEDTRAW: 1970s revival of the FEDSAW movement, in the Transvaal region.

General Law Amendment Act: 1963 law that contained a provision for police to detain suspected political offenders for 90 days without access to lawyers; in practice detainees were often immediately re-detained after release for a further 90 days. Later, the 90 days was amended to 180 days.

Genissimo: maybe a constructed superlative of "genius."

Group Areas Act: 1950 law that, with its many iterations, legislated spatial apartheid (racial segregation). Most of the land and all the best urban and suburban areas were designated "White." Indigenous Africans, Indians and those in the "Coloured" category were squeezed into smaller areas that were poorly located and much less productive.

IDAF: International Defence and Aid Fund for Southern Africa, a fund established in London, England, as an expatriate successor to "Defence and Aid," which had been set up in South Africa to support the accused in political cases but was banned by the government in the 1960s.

Immorality Act: law enacted by the National Party government that criminalised sexual relations between races, as defined by apartheid.

impimpi: a spy, a traitor (Zulu).

Justice and Peace Commission: anti-apartheid mobilisation body originally established by the South African Catholic Bishops' Conference; it later became a multi-faith effort.

Khulumani Support Group: groundbreaking grassroots self-help organisation of victims/survivors of apartheid.

Koevoet: a special forces unit known for its brutality, named after the Afrikaans word for "crowbar."

Komsomol Party School: political training school in Moscow named for the youth wing of the Communist Party of the Soviet Union; it enrolled students from colonised countries as well as the Soviet Union.

lobola: bride price paid by the groom to the bride's family according to South African tradition.

Madiba: Nelson Mandela's clan name, as well as a familiar term of endearment. In South Africa a person may have many names in addition to what Westerners would recognise as a family name; more famous people may have a greater number of different names.

MK: uMkhonto we Sizwe ("Spear of the Nation"), a military structure jointly created in 1961 by the ANC and the South African Communist Party; incorrectly identified as the "armed wing of the ANC."

Morogoro Conference, Tanzania, 1969: conference convened by the ANC to assess problems it had identified after nine years of exile. The conference accepted membership of non-Africans in the ANC; adopted the ANC's first formal Strategy and Tactics document; confirmed the leadership of Oliver Tambo as ANC President and successfully revitalised the organisation.

National Party: the main party of Afrikaner nationalism in South Africa, in power from 1948 to 1994; it invented the term apartheid, and created it as a set of harsh laws and institutions.

Nkosi sikekal i Afrika: "God Bless Africa," a hymn written in 1897 by South Africa's Enoch Sontonga; it is the national anthem of South Africa and some other African countries.

Nomvula: a name (one of Joyce Sikhakhane's names).

OBE: Order of the British Empire, a British award for public service.

Oom Gov: Uncle Gov, the nickname of Govan Mbeki, one of the "Rivonia Triallists" who served time with Nelson Mandela on Robben Island; Govan Mbeki was a distinguished journalist, author and political theorist; his son Thabo Mbeki was President of South Africa, 1999–2008.

PAC: Pan-Africanist Congress, a nationalist, anti-communist grouping that opposed the ANC's Freedom Charter and broke away from the ANC in the late 1950s.

pass laws: the primary instrument by which apartheid was enforced in South Africa. These laws obliged each Black person to carry a dompas at all times that identified the person and recorded where she/he had permission to be; a Black person might be asked to produce this document many times per day and on some days thousands of violators were arrested.

PE: Port Elizabeth.

R11:   Eleven rands, a modest sum of money.

RDP house: rudimentary dwellings created in their millions by the Recon-struction and Development Programme, a social-housing initiative of the post-1994 South African government.

Re roba matsoho: we applaud/congratulate you (Sesotho).

Rivonia Trial 1963/64:   trial of several top leaders of the ANC and the South African Communist Party. In the early 1960s, these two organi-sations set up a clandestine joint headquarters in Rivonia, a suburb of Johannesburg, where they started plotting an armed uprising. In 1963, the police raided the place and made a number of arrests. The Rivo-nia Trial led to life sentences for eight men: Nelson Mandela, Walter Sisulu, Govan Mbeki, Elias Motsoaledi, Andrew Mlangeni, Ahmed Kathrada and Denis Goldberg. All except Goldberg served time on Robben Island.

Robben Island: rocky island lying off the coast of Cape Town in cold, dan-gerous seas that was used as a political prison from the mid-17th cen-tury CE until 1996; Nelson Mandela was held there for 18 years.

SABC: South African Broadcasting Corporation, a state-owned broadcaster.

SACP: South African Communist Party, established in 1921 as the Com-munist Party of South Africa (CPSA); the CPSA was banned in 1950 and was later reconstituted as a clandestine party, the SACP, which was unbanned along with the ANC and the PAC in 1990.

SACTU: South African Congress of Trade Unions, established in 1955; SACTU was a signatory to the Freedom Charter. It was never banned, but its leaders were persecuted and many were driven into exile.

satyagraha: the Hindi-origin term that Gandhi used for non-violent struggle.

SB: Special Branch, the political section of the apartheid-regime police.

Section 10 permit: permit that allowed a Black person to enter an area designated "White" under the Pass Laws, for a limited period and a designated purpose (usually to perform labour).

Sharpeville Massacre, 1960:   massacre that resulted from an action the PAC launched in 1960, to assemble in Sharpeville, a Black-designated area near Johannesburg, and burn their passes; the police opened fire on the crowd, killing 69 and wounding many more.

Siqhwabizandla: we applaud you/ clap hands for you (Xhosa).

sjambokking: a beating with the sjambok, a rhino-hide whip.

Sjoe: an exclamation, pronounced "shoe."

Sobukwe Case: Robert Sobukwe, the leader of the PAC, was imprisoned on Robben Island in 1960. When his prison term expired the govern-ment did not release him but kept him on the island another six years, and later prevented him from leaving the country. The "Sobukwe Case" was an attempt to get permission for him to leave and travel to the US to which Shanthie Naidoo's appeal for permission to leave the country was conjoined. The joining of the cases was to the disadvantage of both.

South African Indian Congress: body that resulted from the merger of two strong local organisations, the Natal Indian Congress and the Transvaal Indian Congress; the SAIC was a signatory of the 1955 Freedom Charter.

Soweto: contraction of "South Western Townships," an area near Johannesburg that under apartheid was designated for Black residents only; Soweto was the biggest and the most populous such area in the country.

TECON: a period in South Africa's freedom struggle when theatre became a valued means of mobilising.

Terrorism Act: legislation passed in 1967 that established BOSS and allowed for detention of suspects on the orders of a senior police officer with no habeas corpus or other rights.

TRC Hearings: the Truth and Reconciliation Commission was established as part of the negotiations in which the ANC and its allies won the ending of apartheid in 1994. It offered amnesty to those who, during apartheid, had committed crimes against humanity in return for those people providing a full public accounting of what they had done and held public hearings in many parts of the country.

tsotsis: young men who hustle; at times, some tsotsis intersected with the political struggle.

UDF: United Democratic Front, a body close to the then-exiled ANC that was established in 1983 to coordinate the work of grassroots groups all over the country; it mobilised large masses of people against apartheid and produced many new leaders. In the early 1990s it disbanded and its members joined ANC structures and leadership.

Urban Bantu Council Act 42: 1961 law that established a small degree of token self-management, but actually indirect rule, in urban townships.

USIS: United States Information Service, a governmental body that sometimes provides cover for intelligence operations.

veld: usually refers to rural land that is not cultivated.

Walmer: suburb of Port Elizabeth.

Yena nowakwakha: she and her spouse (Nguni: Zulu or Xhosa).

Prologue

6 April 2018 – Pretoria Central Prison

It is 4 am and dark, apart from a few dim light bulbs dotted around pathways. April's autumn wind chills Gauteng, but the shivers that come and go this morning are not just from the crisp air. We are at the old gallows of Pretoria Central Prison. Cold steel, swaying nooses and an eerie breeze keeps everyone quiet. It is as if the memories, the spirits, of all the lives that were snuffed out here still linger.

The death of Winnie Mandela just four days before is on all of our minds and she is part of the reason why photographer Alon Skuy and I are here. We are in search of a narrative about her incarceration in a cell in this building in the 1960s and 1970s to include in the *Sunday Times'* coverage of her death and memorials.

But it is the anniversary of another death that we are commemorating and remembering today, that of Solomon Mahlangu, the MK (uMkhonto we Sizwe ("Spear of the Nation")) freedom fighter who was hanged here on 6 April 1979. It is a sombre but low-key annual family ritual – the re-enactment of his final walk, 39 steps, to the gallows. The last words he uttered were: "My blood will nourish the tree that will bear the fruits of freedom. Tell my people that I love them. They must continue the fight."

The gallows were equipped to hang seven people at once, but historians record that the 22-year-old was alone the morning he was hanged, at 6 am, as the dawn sun was lightening the sky.

The young recruit, fresh out of the ANC's (African National Congress's) military training camps in Angola and Swaziland, had been tasked with crossing the border into South Africa with grenades and pamphlets. The Mamelodi student, new to politics and impassioned by the '76 riots, was so green that he and a friend were easily detected for "acting suspiciously" not long after arriving in Johannesburg. A gun battle with police ensued, in which a bystander was shot, though not clearly, by Mahlangu. It earned him the death sentence. This young life, lost tragically to the struggle against apartheid, is just one of so many atrocities of the era.

DOI: 10.4324/9781003228905-1

As he was led to his execution, Mahlangu would have been walked past the women's cell block, which, ten years before, had been the home of Winnie Mandela and six other extraordinary women for close to two years.

After the ceremony, the prison authorities had promised to allow us time to locate the women's cells and so avoid the red tape of seeking permission to access the high-security space on another day.

Now named Kgosi Mampuru II Correctional Centre, the historic and still functioning prison at the corner of Wimbledon and Klawer streets in Salvokop is made up of a number of imposing, flat and khaki-coloured buildings on the outskirts of Pretoria's central business district. Here, political prisoners were kept among murderers and thieves. It was large enough for prisoners to disappear, particularly in the maze of solitary cells reserved for political detainees.

As the light starts to warm the day after the Mahlangu ceremony, we arrive at the red brick walls surrounded by green lawns and roses near the warders' tennis court and sparkling swimming pool, a stark contrast to the vicious, dark days the precinct had seen during the apartheid years.

We walk along the cobblestones in search of Winnie's cell – looking for the grey, blood-splattered walls she'd described in her secret diary – but if we expected to find it as she described it, we are disappointed. We come instead to a stone wall. All that remains of the original building, which dates from 1906, is a singular brownstone wall and a turret, preserved as a heritage structure. We are told that the building had been completely renovated and restyled several times since 1969.

One of the prison's directors, Rudie Koekemoer, tells us it now houses day-parole and medium-security male prisoners. It has bigger windows, linoleum floors, a TV lounge and cells with cupboards in them, and toilets. "We tried to find the warders who might have been here when she was here, but many have died or retired," Koekemoer says. Like much of apartheid-era documentation, records would have been destroyed and officers of the time went silently into retirement or their graves.

The Department of Correctional Services has few details of the women's time in solitary, because they were detainees, not inmates. They had not been convicted of a crime; they were not prisoners who had been charged and were awaiting trial, even though they were detained for that lengthy period. Many would not have received prison numbers.

"From what she described from her window, her cell would have been on the east side, but the entire building (apart from the heritage wall) was renovated," Koekemoer points out. "There is no solitary confinement anymore."

From the winter of 1969 through to the spring of 1970, in conditions so inhospitable that Winnie became gravely ill, she and the six other women who were held here, each in her tiny cement-floored cell, were removed only for sessions of interrogation and torture. Despite their solitary confinement, they stood together in spirit. Everything else around them was aimed at their demise, in physical form or otherwise. An excerpt from Winnie's prison memoirs reads:

> I am next to the assault chamber. As long as I live I shall never forget the nightmares I have suffered as a result of the daily prisoners' piercing screams as the brutal corporal punishment is inflicted on them. As the cane lashes at them, sometimes a hose pipe, you feel it tearing at your own flesh mercilessly. It's hard to imagine women inflicting so much punishment. I have shed tears ... unconsciously and often forget even to wipe them off.
>
> These hysterical screams pierce through my heart and injure my dignity so much. The hero of these assaults is barely 23-years-old, very often the screaming voice appealing for mercy is that of a mother twice her age but of course she is white, a matron (at) that, this qualifies her for everything. The prisoner is at her mercy, life and all. She even bangs their heads against my cell wall in her fury. As the blood spurts from the gaping wounds she hits harder.[1]

It is an icy morning. We join the other members of the media who have gathered for refreshments. Everyone is chatting about Winnie, sharing the stories that have surfaced in the few days since her death and discussing the impending funeral arrangements.

I accept a hot mug of tea and warm my fingers around it.

Note

1 Madikizela-Mandela, 2013.

1 The legacy of trauma

They say trauma lives in our DNA. It's simple science, really. We are made up of many parts of microscopic bits. Some of these parts are physical, and others exist on a different level – subtle, intangible parts, in the form of memories, emotions and experiences.

When I think of the lived experiences of the women in this story, I realise that perhaps there is a scientific explanation for why I feel so deeply connected to them and their histories, even though we were born generations apart. Why I feel this in my gut, in a tightening at my throat, in overwhelming sadness.

When you consider a history like South Africa's and witness the psychological mess we're in today, why, I have to ask, do South Africans not honour and respect those who suffered for justice and freedom as it is set out for us in the constitution?

> Honour those who suffered for justice and freedom in our land;
> Respect those who have worked to build and develop our country;
>> Heal the divisions of the past and establish a society based on democratic values, social justice and fundamental human rights.

If they are in our DNA, and it is mandated in our foundation document, these solemn words should at the very least be in our consciousness as we walk this sweet, flawed path of democracy together.

Democracy. This was not an ethereal concept, something that was yearned for to change our way of life, even though it might have felt like one. And yes, we may have a surface of democracy now, and slivers of light do shine through, but what about the deep, dark substrata below? When we ask, What went wrong? How did we get here? How could such a long road turn onto this path? Perhaps one of the answers is that too few of us have the will to dig deeper, to penetrate those layers enough to shift our perspectives.

Fifty years prior to the writing of this book, a certain political trial – which was known as the Trial of 22 – impacted the country's history not by an outcome, but by the absence of one. It steered the revolution against

DOI: 10.4324/9781003228905-2

apartheid in a direction which subtly altered the road to democracy and the dismantling of the apartheid system of segregation. This trial, and others that came before and after it in the long, long struggle, may give us clues to why anger, hurt and unresolved trauma show up fresh and raw as a new wound five decades, a lifetime, later.

If we have to consider bookends to the struggle for freedom in South Africa, starting with Passive Resistance and ending with Armed Resistance, there are reams of stories in between. Along the way were the Women's March of 1956, the 1960 State of Emergency, the Sharpeville massacre in 1960, the Soweto uprising in 1976 ... years and years until freedom arrived. What happened, every day, though? What filled the minutiae of the minutes and days that went on and on for those years?

The Trial of 22 or, as the record would read, *The State versus Ndou and 21 others*, fits halfway through the story, in 1969. What happened – or didn't happen – in that courtroom in the Old Synagogue in Pretoria was quietly momentous. It was this trial that edged the movement on towards the ultimate goal, freedom, and yet there is little known or written about it.

It began on 14 October 1969. There were 22 accused, men and women, arraigned before the Supreme Court on 21 charges under the Suppression of Communism Act.

Among the 22 were seven women: Nomzamo Winnie Mandela, Martha Dhlamini, Thokozile Mngoma, Rita Ndzanga, Nondwe Mankahla, Joyce Sikhakhane and Shanthie Naidoo.

It was in April 2018, while reporting for the *Sunday Times* on Winnie Mandela's death, that I first read about the trial. It turned out that four of the women, all of them then in their 80s, were not only still alive but they had attended Winnie's funeral. Rita Ndzanga, a tiny woman with a waning, husky voice, and wearing a headscarf in African National Congress (ANC) colours, delivered one of the many eulogies. The women were quoted in an article or two in the media, and then they went back home to their respective quiet lives.

I wanted to know who these women were, these friends and comrades of Winnie Mandela. What had brought them together at that moment in 1969 and what happened to them afterwards?

Martha Dhlamini and Thokozile Mngoma had since passed on, but I made contact with each of the four remaining women and asked if I could visit them. They promised time when the dust had settled. The lengthy funeral proceedings had taken their toll. They first needed to rest.

****

Fatigue hung over the funeral in another form. Working on a Sunday newspaper, as the coverage of Winnie Mandela's passing unfolded, I experienced prickles of unease. Within a few minutes of her death on Monday, 2 April 2018, the electronic daily press was telling the basic story: that she had died at the age of 81; that she was a diabetic who had recently undergone several major surgeries; that she had been in poor health. Then, towards the latter part of the week, bits of hell bubbled up.

When international media picked up on the story, that "the wife of Nelson Mandela" had died, my sense was perhaps that that particular context was needed for global audiences, but the prickles soon turned to full-on rage at how the media chose to remind the world who Winnie was: the fraud charges that were brought against her came up, as did her troubled past and a wayward youth. In fact, everything from guerrilla warfare to extra-marital affairs, not forgetting murder, filled media platforms. One South African editorial alluded to Winnie being inebriated and with "not-so-good" people at the time of Mandela's release in 1990, and questioned why anyone would emulate her. They offered many faces of Winnie Mandela, without revealing which face was actually hers, but it seemed that history was in danger of relegating her to a philandering drunk turned militant ex-wife.

But then, the social media heavens opened – you cannot die in peace in the era of social media – and in one of those rare moments it showed up as a force for good.

Journalist Kyle Findlay analysed some 700,000 tweets which showed that the early conversation around her death was

> dominated by left-leaning communities who saw Winnie as a militant martyr who was not appreciated in her time and who was the victim of under-handed machinations, both by the apartheid government and by more moderate members of her own party, the African National Congress, the South African liberation movement.[1]

Many writers, and female writers in particular, stood up against the pejorative narrative and demanded that Winnie's contribution be recognised.

Researcher Shireen Hassim described how women in the ANC were marginalised from its powerful decision-making structures. She questioned the stereotypes, particularly around Winnie.

> Unlike male leaders, her personal life was constantly under the spotlight (no doubt aided by a zealous security machinery that kept her under constant surveillance), and she was judged harshly and unfairly for her private choices. Although she was a masterful player of the familial categories of wife and mother, she felt reduced by them too.[2]

One of the things I wanted to ask of her detention mates and compatriots, the women with whom she had been jailed and tortured while taking up roles left by the imprisoned male leadership in the 1960s and beyond, was what they thought of how the media was portraying Winnie's legacy. The answer was that they were incensed. Ma Rita included the publication I worked for in the "cruel media" in her anger and refused to speak to me for months afterwards.

Winnie's death reminds us that the female narrative of the struggle against apartheid, and in history, is vastly different to that of the male, and either we are not aware of it or we do not acknowledge the extent of it. What of the emotional impact on women like Winnie Mandela and the six other women who had been held with her at the same time prior to that 1969 trial? What led to Winnie's "behaviour" in subsequent decades? What must it have been like every day in the firing line while male leaders were absent?

Earlier in 2018, at the annual commemoration of the late Rivonia triallist Ahmed Kathrada's death, the question of missing *her*stories was raised. In a video recorded shortly before his death in 2017, which was played at the tribute, Kathrada said that his life partner Barbara Hogan, a former minister, former detainee, had not told her story of incarceration and struggle, and he believed it was time. She avoided the question, but it was not the first time it had been raised. HIV advocacy group the Treatment Action Campaign (TAC) some years before (2010) had published a brief ode to Hogan, saying: "When Barbara was appointed Minister of Health in 2008, most people did not know her. This tribute is written because she is a remarkable (almost anonymous) leader."

At the 2020 inquest into the death of Dr Neil Aggett, an anti-apartheid activist who died on 5 February 1982 while in detention after being arrested by the South African security police, Hogan gave rare testimony about her own detention in a public space. "Can I just say that the reopening of the inquest (from 1982) is very painful for everyone sitting here, but it's timely and I have just spoken of the terrors that I faced and many people faced worse," said Hogan. "Neil and everyone who died in detention under these terrible circumstances needs to have justice, needs to be heard and have justice done."[3]

Hogan was detained in 1981. She was held in solitary for a year, then at trial convicted under the Suppression of Communism Act and sentenced to ten years in prison. "I was desperate," Hogan said of her period in detention.

> I wanted to kill myself. I saw no way of my getting out of that situation because I knew of many people who died in detention. I had friends who had been tortured very badly at John Vorster Square. I knew what they (the apartheid security police) were capable of and I just saw myself being tortured to death for information I simply could not provide.

She had tried to commit suicide by stealing the medication prescribed for her injuries, swallowing it all and tying the cord from her dressing gown around her neck.

Hers is one of many stories of women like her, activists working for justice, journalists, wives of imprisoned cadres and the female struggle leaders themselves. The women who participated in the movement are ageing now, and many have passed on. But there are a few who can share the stories of what happened in their minds and to their bodies when they were targeted by the apartheid government systematically to break down the machinery that ran on the convictions of those who believed so steadfastly in it that they would risk their lives and their families. The effects would last for years to come.

These women lived through harassment and abuse that was gender specific. Academic research by Professor Kalpana Hiralal at the University of KwaZulu-Natal reveals how female political detainees were treated particularly harshly. Gender sensitivity was considered a secondary weapon.

Strip searches conducted by male officers, threats and acts of sexual assault – inspection of every orifice by male officers alone in their cells; political prisoners told that their children would be murdered; denial of sanitary material – these were meant to batter women as fiercely as possible, attacking them at their womanhood. Hiralal described how

> pregnant women were threatened with drinking poison by their captors, another had her breasts slammed in a drawer, repeatedly. The nature of women's incarceration, interrogation, and the impact on their personal lives highlights not only the gendered aspects of imprisonment but also the heterogeneity of women's experiences. Apartheid prisons imposed brutal and inhumane prison conditions that denigrated and humiliated women, thus becoming a site of humiliation.[4]

But the worst, many women would say, was denial of visits from or news of their children.

Despite these conditions, women were far from compliant. Hiralal wrote

> They negotiated their confined spaces through common sense, tenacity and a steadfast belief in their resistance and the justice of their struggle. The courage and sacrifices they made are important in giving greater visibility to both the tangible and intangible contributions women made in the liberation struggle in South Africa. The gendered prison narratives illustrate not only women's contributions to the liberation struggle in their own right but also how the prison was another terrain of political struggle, resistance, confrontation, and negotiation by women,[5]

There are suggestions that political prisoners have lived with untreated post-traumatic stress disorder (PTSD). Writing in a paper entitled "Truth and Memory" for the Khulumani Support Group for people harmed by apartheid, *Wendy Isaack* wrote: "… the political compromises made in the South African transition failed to address violence against women and have left women vulnerable and victimised."[6]

For me personally, visions of young women ripped from their lives, their families, mothers taken away by police while their young children watched, are haunting and I don't believe I am alone in feeling haunted by such images. If we pause to think about these women's children, with long-absent fathers and routinely missing mothers, we may get an inkling of what wounds the current and subsequent generations of South Africans are still having to bear. If, as the science says, we carry them in our DNA, a deeper exploration will allow a deeper understanding. Few of the older generation have sought psychological help for the emotional trauma they suffered as a result of standing up for their political beliefs. It is my view that the outcomes continue to be reflected in South African society today.

In reading up on the Trial of 22 as much as I could in advance of meeting with the four remaining women who went through it, I soon realised that there is lean and scattered information about it. The bare facts were there, and the court record, which is a terse and unenlightening thing. I was banking on the women still having vivid memories of those harsh months 50 years later and being willing to tell me about them. I had interviewed them each telephonically for the news reports following Winnie's death, but there was more of the story to tell.

I believed that if I was able to talk to these women, whose lives had been bound inextricably together in the late 1960s, the insights they might be able to offer of that time and their experiences at the hands of the notorious special branch would be a gift that I would not take lightly. I wanted to get to know them, to hear their stories, to better understand the context and the times.

Notes

1 Findlay, 2018.
2 Hassim, 2018.
3 Hogan, 2020.
4 Hiralal, 2015.
5 Hiralal, 2015.
6 Isaack, Khulumani Support Group, n.d.

2 Finding the women

It is important to understand the context of the Trial of 22. During the 1960s, the "second phase" of apartheid, which was when the separatist laws were deeply entrenched, the oppressive government increased the police force and gave more power to law enforcement by passing the General Law Amendment Act of 1963 – or 90-day detention law. This meant that lengthy and unsubstantiated detentions were written into law. The power of the state control at the time was described as fortified and brutal. The intention was to capture and silence those who were the driving forces behind the liberation struggle. The period was benchmarked by the Rivonia Trial, at the end of which the ANC (African National Congress) leadership was sentenced to life imprisonment on Robben Island in 1963/64.

The late ANC leader Govan Mbeki wrote how after the Rivonia arrests, the security police "threw a wide dragnet in which they collected a large number of known activists. In the course of detention, some … broke down."

> The ANC took a hard knock, which threw it into disarray and from which it took some years to recover. The number of ANC members who were on Robben Island during the (1960s) and the number of women ANC members, especially from Port Elizabeth and Cradock, who served in various jails in the Transvaal, were an indication of the extent to which the organisation had been crippled. Worse still, when they were released after serving short sentences of two-and-a-half years to five and ten years, further charges were trumped up by the police. Thereafter they were sent back to jail to serve longer periods of imprisonment, or else they were endorsed out of the urban areas to … desolate places …[1]

Mbeki wrote that the organisation was weakened.

> It is quite understandable why after such a vicious attack by the government, the organisation had to reorganise and re-group before it could launch its activities again. One of the most significant features of the

DOI: 10.4324/9781003228905-3

period was the convening of the Morogoro Conference in (Tanzania) in 1967 at which a decision was taken to open membership of the ANC to all who shared its policies, irrespective of colour or race. This decision marked a new era in that the major national liberation organisation became non-racial.[2]

In 1969 it had been six years since the Rivonia Trial. During all that time, with the male leaders imprisoned, long before the larger body became "non-racial," the women who remained behind had been at the coalface of the struggle. They were friends and comrades, carrying themselves and the organisation covertly. Ordinary women, with children and jobs, hopes and dreams. Their reality was years of harassment, long periods of detention, isolation, torture and abuse.

Their stories have largely gone undetected, untold, in the shadow of the mainstream narrative – that of the Rivonia triallists and Robben Island political prisoners. Some stories have been unsympathetically told, as in the case of Winnie Mandela. Perhaps these women wanted it this way, to be silent contributors, and that is the reason why we know only a handful of their stories or even who they were. The impact on the individual women we may never know, but South African society is likely always to feel it collectively. It is, after all, in our DNA.

Winnie might have been the figurehead, but there were countless others. In 2018, when much was being written about her life and death, the feeling was that she had "multiplied" as women rallied together. Back then, they *were* multiples, hundreds if not thousands of women who shared the strength and the pain of a common experience during the struggle. There were women's movements around the country which made remarkable impact.

Years after her detention in 1969, Winnie wrote:

> When I was in detention for all those months, my two children nearly died. When I came out they were so lean; they had had such a hard time. They were covered in sores, malnutrition sores. And they wonder why I am like I am. And they have a nerve to say, "Oh Madiba is such a peaceful person, you know. We wonder how he had such a wife who is so violent?"

The leadership on Robben Island was never touched; the leadership on Robben Island had no idea what it was like to engage the enemy physically. The leadership was removed and cushioned behind prison walls; they had their three meals a day.

> In fact, ironically, we must thank the authorities for keeping our leadership alive; they were not tortured. They did not know what we were talking about and when we were reported to be so violent, engaged in the physical struggle, fighting the Boers underground, they did not

understand because none of them had ever been subjected to that, not even Madiba himself – they never touched him, they would not have dared. We were the foot soldiers.[3]

The trial was mentioned in some of the eulogies at Winnie Mandela's funeral, reminding the country that about 50 years before, these 22, which included 7 women, were tortured by the apartheid government's security branch and held in solitary confinement, without sight of their families, for days, weeks, months ... For nearly two years, deprived of sensory experiences, they were held in small, single cells.

There are hints and allusions to post-traumatic stress experienced by those involved in the struggle for liberation. It was a long-drawn-out fight that spanned generations in its effect. But the specific focus on the women in this trial is because history tells us that female experience of political activism and detention was vastly different from that of the men. Gender-specific violence, emotional torture – even the manner in which they are remembered – is important in understanding the past and present South Africa, and the country's collective mental state.

The activism of women in the struggle against apartheid was vital. Women took on central political roles where gaps were left by imprisoned male leaders. They took on additional political roles to their personal ones, abandoning the societal expectation of motherhood and nurturing, or in spite of it. These mothers, daughters and sisters who contributed and fought on the streets even after their release are important. Their bodies and minds were tortured in unimaginable ways, their own children used as collateral against them. Few remember debriefing or any kind of counselling. They were too busy fighting the long fight, surviving.

The women who were kept at Pretoria Central Prison were detained precisely in order to be broken. Every detail of their time in prison was malevolently concocted. From the beautiful gardens they could see out of the cracks of their cell walls, with manicured grass lawns and roses on one end to the gallows on the other. They were purposely placed close enough to see freedom, and where they would be able to hear their comrades and common criminals alike wail while walking to their assault or death.

They kept their minds busy in any way they could, sewing and re-sewing the hems of their skirts, folding and refolding their meagre linen, walking the few steps between concrete walls as exercise, anything to keep their minds away from what they did not know: who in their families was dead or alive, whether their children had eaten that day, if they were doing their homework.

Winnie Mandela's story is well known and well documented, but many stories of the other women who chose to get involved and suffered horribly in detention and prison for their courage and convictions are hardly known at all. As that generation ages and memories fade, their prison experience and what they did afterwards, building a resistance movement that is known worldwide, is fading too.

The year 2019/20 marked the 50th anniversary of the detention of those of the Trial of 22, and the stories of the seven women involved has not thus far been told collectively or in the context of their emotional experience. They would not have known then, but hopefully we do now, that in surviving detention and standing up for their comrades in the Trial of 22 they bravely paved the path to democracy.

Sadly, the personal stories of Martha Dhlamini and Thokozile "Venus" Mngoma have gone with them to the grave. They were older than the others and would have been matriarchal to the younger women. While it is known that the two remained active in their community in Alexandra township, there is fragmented information about their lives, and their time in detention.

That they were heroines, there is little doubt.

Former president Thabo Mbeki invited Martha to a Women's Day event in 2006, the 50th Anniversary of the 1956 Women's March, held at the Union Buildings in Tshwane. Mbeki said in his address:

> Martha Dhlamini remains to this day a freedom fighter, having refused to be broken by the detentions and the banning orders that the apartheid regime thought would destroy her determination to see the women and people of our country liberated from the yoke of racist oppression.[4]

He recalled a speech she had made in Alexandra in which she described her journey. She became actively involved in politics in the late 1950s, organising a protest for women during the Potato Boycott, against the abuse of labourers on potato farms in Bethal in the former Eastern Transvaal (now Mpumalanga).

Martha was an early member of the Federation of South African Women (FEDSAW), which organised the 1956 Women's March to the Union Buildings in Pretoria against the introduction of the apartheid pass laws for black women. She was also a key figure in the presentation of a petition to the then Prime Minister JG Strijdom. The nationwide mobilisation against pass laws for women on 9 August 1956 is now celebrated as Women's Day in South Africa. Along with women leaders Helen Joseph, Rahima Moosa, Sophie Williams-De Bruyn and Lillian Ngoyi, they headlined the protest of 20,000 fellow South African women.

She was dedicated to the women's movement. In her speech, Martha said: "We organised demonstrations in town under the leadership of Lillian Ngoyi and Helen Joseph. We were arrested and taken to Number 4 prison." Nelson Mandela was their legal representative. After they were discharged Martha was arrested again in 1960 when "the government swooped the whole country" – this was during the state of emergency which saw 18,000 people arrested. "I was taken again to Number 4 prison."[5]

Now part of the Constitution Hill Human Rights precinct in Braamfontein, Number 4 and Number 5 prisons were where black prisoners were held; the precinct includes the Old Fort, 11 Kotze Street, which housed white prisoners, yet another manifestation of apartheid separation, and the apex court, the Constitutional Court. Referring to Number 4 and Number 5, the Constitution Hill exhibition reads:

> These sections held large communal cells that were overcrowded, rife with disease, and gang violence. Food was rationed according to racial groups, with African men receiving the smallest and least nutritious portions. Former political prisoners incarcerated at Number 4 include Mahatma Gandhi, the Indian civil rights leader; Robert Sobukwe, founder of the Pan Africanist Congress; and Albert Luthuli, former ANC president.

It was a horrid place, where women were not allowed to wash for weeks on end. Typhoid fever raged through the prison community. A disturbing story was that of activist Phila Ndwandwe, who was tortured and kept naked for ten days before she was assassinated. Before her death, Ndwandwe reportedly fashioned underwear for herself out of a scrap of blue plastic, in an attempt at some dignity. The plastic underwear was installed as an artistic symbol in the precinct.

Martha Dhlamini was also a member of the original Congress of the People, which adopted the Freedom Charter. The historic document pledged to continue the struggle until a new democratic order was put in place. It was a concrete wish list for the country, following the doctrine that "South Africa belongs to all who live in it" and that "all shall be equal before the law."[6]

Part of her duties, along with those of Thoko and others, would have been the house-to-house campaign in Alexandra township, listening to the demands of the people which were later incorporated in the document.

As a banned person, Martha's activism was curtailed.

> In 1964 I was put under the banning order for fifteen years by the Minister of Justice, John Vorster. I was ordered to report at Bramley police station every Monday between 7 am and 5 pm. When (fellow activist) Florence Mophosho left the country, I was ordered to leave with her but, because my children were too young, I did not go.[7]

The banning order gave her little room for movement: "I was not allowed to have visitors or to attend any gathering. When my first born got married, I went to Pretoria to ask for permission to attend the wedding."[8] The government prevented banned people from attending funerals and weddings, which were considered public gatherings.

And, in line with the charges of the Trial of 22, she was an "organiser" for the ANC and participated in many of the resistance campaigns of that time.

Rita Ndzanga recalled Martha being assaulted in prison during their detention. Winnie Mandela stopped a security officer from hurting her, incensed by the assault of her elder. "You dare touch her, you dare touch that woman!" she said, and the officer retreated, although threatening her with violence.

After her release, Martha spent her time in active work as far as banning would allow her, along with her comrade, Thoko.

Thoko, similarly, was a founding member of FEDSAW. She also helped form the Alexandra Women's Organisation (AWO), after the ANC and the leaders of FEDSAW were banned in 1960. Under AWO, women would secretly convene at Mngoma's house, hiding from the security branch. These movements, along with many others, were all monitored by the security police and constantly under surveillance. This led to her arrest in 1969.

While Thoko remained a banned person and was confined to her home in the 1980s she remained very much an activist. She shared oral histories with young revolutionaries, and, in 1983 she was involved in the founding of the United Democratic Front (UDF), the umbrella organisation of anti-apartheid movements and civic groups. She was also part of the funerals network – when burials became the meeting ground for the organisers, posing as caterers and mourners.

Thoko died in 1995 at her home in Alex, a year after the first democratic elections.

In 2012, a plaque was unveiled in her memory at a Marlboro clinic named after her, the Thoko Mngoma Clinic. According to the City of Johannesburg's official website, residents of Alexandra came in their numbers to honour the woman considered by many to be "the mother of the community, an organiser and a revolutionary."

****

It was by chance and fortuitous timing that I could meet the remaining four women from the trial, in person, in the ensuing months after Winnie Mandela's funeral. It meant travelling between Johannesburg and Port Elizabeth, to Soweto and Pretoria, to piece together the portions of the story where their lives intersected nearly five decades prior.

During the process, as time went by, I was keenly aware that these remarkable women were ageing. I noticed that their memories sometimes became fragmented, that their health was deteriorating. It became urgent to hear their personal stories but also to find their families, some of whom were scattered across the world, in the hope that they could add detail to their rich contributions, what the women sometimes dismissed as "duty" and stopped there.

You will, I hope, have noticed my name – Shanthini Naidoo. Let me say at the outset that it is purely coincidental – not a literary device, as one of the early editors thought – that I do share a name or a derivative of it, with

Shanthie Naidoo. There is no bloodline between us of which I am aware. But the connection of our names provided coincidence upon coincidence. Shanthie is retired now and lives in Johannesburg; she returned to South Africa from the UK after 1994. She is one of the reasons why this story found me, and I am glad for it. It felt destined.

Joyce Sikhakhane-Rankin agreed to speak to me almost by mistake or perhaps charmed by the confusion about her friend with the similar name. And the same for Joyce's children, who thought I was a granddaughter of their mother's good friend, whom they had never met. For Nondwe and Ma Rita, it was a memory trigger, hearing a name from a story they hadn't revisited for many years. And the coincidence brought a unique way into their homes and minds. For this, I am thankful for a name that has been mispronounced all of my adult life. That connection binds me to Shanthie Naidoo in a way that is inspiring, but mostly because she lives her *shanthi* (peace) more than any other human being I have met.

Notes

1 Mbeki, 1994.
2 Mbeki, 1994.
3 Madikizela-Mandela, 2013.
4 Mbeki, 2006.
5 Dhlamini, 2006.
6 Dhlamini, 2006.
7 Dhlamini, 2006.
8 Dhlamini, 2006.

3 The trial

They were alleged to have inspected trains and railway installations in the Johannesburg area to find targets for sabotage and to have arranged visits to prisons – including Robben Island, where Mr. Mandela is imprisoned – in connection with National Congress business, to have worked with others in arranging financial aid and assistance to the organization, to have arranged to have contact with "guerrilla fighters" and to have "encouraged feelings of hostility between the races."

New York Times, February 1970

The Old Synagogue in Pretorius Street was repurposed as a court of apartheid. Designed in the architectural traditions of the Eastern Roman Empire in 1897, this was the first Jewish house of worship to be consecrated in Pretoria. After 1952, the Department of Public Works ensured that the building had lost all sense of God; even the windows were boarded up to remove evidence of devotion or beauty.

The space allowed for relatively large numbers, and batches of political prisoners stood trial there over the years for "communist acts" ranging from sabotage to collection of alms for the families of political prisoners by missionaries. Security was tight. Members of the special branch were always in attendance and police officers, armed to the teeth, stood outside with machine-guns. Women were not allowed to carry handbags into the building. While it was far off from Johannesburg, families and comrades arrived in numbers, setting up tea and food stalls, singing songs of protest and support, congregating in the streets outside.

Although most of the 22 men and women who stood in the dock in the Old Synagogue that summer's day in 1969 were unfamiliar to one another, they knew who they were. They were the scaffolding of the anti-apartheid movement – a motley collection, joined together by a common cause.

How they had got there was the result of a large-scale, staggered but finely coordinated national raid on the part of the South African security police during the cold early winter months of April and May. Almost all of them

DOI: 10.4324/9781003228905-4

had been pulled out of their homes at ungodly hours by the special branch and taken away from their families. To all intents and purposes, they simply disappeared.

An International Defence and Aid Fund (IDAF) document which captured the details from the detainees afterwards noted:

> In each home, police searched for many hours, and took away with them books, private letters, newspaper cuttings, typewriters, and many things which had nothing to do with politics, or which were political, but legal. Some of those arrested were journalists and writers, one was a poet, some were students.[1]
>
> The police took drafts of short stories, poetry, articles; copies of the London *Observer*; student magazines; love letters. Security officers testified to finding a number of books, none of which were banned, and press cuttings in the house of one of the accused, a 19-year-old student, Joseph Sikalala. They also recovered two school notebooks in which, in addition to algebraic equations, there were some notes. In all the forty, perhaps fifty, homes raided during May and June, the total of "subversive" documents seemed to be a copy of a pamphlet issued by the ANC in London, and one or two documents said to relate to the ANC.[2]

The accused would have made a pathetic picture in the courtroom, some in the same set of clothes they'd been wearing when they were taken. Some were skeletal; most were sallow skinned from the lack of decent food and exercise, sunlight and fresh air. More than a few bore scars and bruises from the physical torture they'd endured.

They were charged under the Suppression of Communism Act 1950 (Act 44 of 1950)[3] for, in layman's terms, terrorism and treason. Of the seven women on trial, two were to be called as state witnesses.

Among the lawyers for the defence were George Bizos, Sydney Kentridge and Joel Carlson.

The names of the 22 were recorded as[4]

Mr. Samson Ratshivande Ndou
Mr. David Motau
Mrs. Nonzoma Winnie Mandela
Mr. Hiengani Jackson Mahlaule
Mr. Elliot Goldberg Tshabangu
Miss Joyce Nomala Sikhakhane
Mr. Nanko Paulus Matshaba
Mr. Lawrence Ndzanga
Mrs. Rita Anita Ndzanga
Mr. Joseph Sikalala
Mr. David Dalton Tsotetsi
Mr. Victor Emmanuel Mazitulela

Mr. George Mokwebo
Mr. Joseph Chamberlain Nobanda
Mr. Simon Mosikare
Mr. Douglas Mtshetshe Mvembe
Miss Venus Thokozile Mngoma
Miss Martha Dhlamini
Mr. Owen Msimilele Vanqa
Mr. Livingstone Mancoko
Mr. Peter Zexforth [sic] Magubane
Mr. Samuel Solomon Pholotho

The detainees were taken to Pretoria from all around the country, some journeys longer than others, where they were held in solitary confinement and worked on by operatives to create evidence for this trial. In terms of apartheid law, they could be held for 90 days without being charged, without access to lawyers.

Weeks and then months passed. Winter turned to spring. On the other side of the world, in the US, the music festival that came to be known as Woodstock was taking place, a gathering of peace and unity and harmony in protest against the controversial Vietnam War. While this outdoor demonstration by half a million peace-loving people made news around the world, it could not have been further from the oppression that was happening in South Africa at the same time. Locked away, their personal freedom brutally taken from them, with no news from the outside world, and no visitors allowed, the detained persons in their cells could scarcely tell day from night. They were taken from their cells at any time only to be interrogated and tortured by men and women trained to make their incarceration unbearable.

Among the detainees, three young men died soon after their arrest – Michael Shivute, on the night of his detention, Caleb Mayekiso, 19 days later, and the Imam Abdullah Haron, four months after being detained.

Only when the summer heat was dry and stifling would the 22 see daylight again, on trial in the Old Synagogue. They sat in the dock, hearing themselves being described as guerrillas, spies and terrorists. What they were, in reality, were ordinary people – activists, trade unionists, "organisers," individual cogs in the network of messengers, pamphlet distributors and social workers trying to support the oppressed population. They did have a singular motive, however: freedom for South Africa.

In the courtroom constables armed with automatic pistols at the ready sat behind the rows of the accused. Dishevelled and dispirited, in worn-out clothing and obviously in strained health, by now the prisoners were shadows of their former selves. Their families had last seen them nearly a year before, and the toll of poor food rations and lack of medical care, eyesight affected by being kept away in freezing dungeons, would have been visible.

They might have wondered who their fellow captives were and where they were from. Perhaps they would have recognised voices from hushed, stolen midnight discussions. Many were from the Eastern Cape, some from the Transvaal, and all had been gathered up by the security police who had tenuously linked them, accused and witnesses.

Prosecutor JH Liebenberg addressed the court. He claimed that the accused had revived the African National Congress (ANC) in 1967 and established contact among old comrades. Meetings had been held "in houses, in cars and in the veld," where groups were instructed in ANC policy.

There was evidence that the ANC was an integral part of the communist movement in South Africa, he continued. This evidence came in the form of pamphlets which could be traced back to the ANC London office for distribution in South Africa and spoke of "guerrilla warfare" to be instigated by members of the ANC, the South African Communist Party and the South African Indian Congress. Examples were presented to the court. Which of the triallists were responsible for the distribution of these pamphlets, however, was not made clear. Other charges impossible to prove in law were presented, from showing support for freedom fighters and providing social welfare for the families of political prisoners, to considering armed uprising and military training.

Records read:

> (A witness) Eselina Klaas from Port Elizabeth said she had distributed forms to families of six people who had been released from jail after serving sentences for ANC activities, and that she had delivered the completed forms to Mrs. Ndzanga, in Johannesburg, Mrs. Ndzanga and Mrs. Mandela gave her R11 and some old clothing to distribute to people in financial difficulties.[5]

Liebenberg claimed the 22 "frequently" visited Nelson Mandela and others in prison, and that Mandela had shared instructions around communism. The first claim was an inane accusation, and one which commentators abroad wrote scathingly about – prisoners on Robben Island were allowed one visitor twice a year, and few could have afforded the travel to the Cape or were banned from travelling outside their magisterial districts.

The prosecutor continued: "In the home of Mr. and Mrs. Ndzanga the police had found press cuttings on the lack of school facilities for African children, and on other matters; and a photograph of Mr. Ndzanga giving the (Amandla) salute."[6] Evidence against Winnie Mandela, Joyce Sikhakhane and Rita Ndzanga included that they had "duplicated a leaflet one Sunday in March of 1968. The leaflet, issued in the name of the ANC, exhorted the people not to be hoodwinked into accepting the Urban Bantu Council (Act), as a form of freedom."[7] The women also duplicated a message of farewell to a Mr Lekoto, to be read at his funeral. "Mrs. Mandela," Liebenberg told the court, "had a profound knowledge of communism. She had read works by Lenin, Trotsky and Che Guevara and had expressed a great interest in Zhivago's *History of Russia*."[8] This information had been supplied by a "friend," Maud Katzenellenbogen.

Thirty-two-year-old Shanthie Naidoo was surprised to hear her name being called as a state witness. She had been detained a month or two after the initial raids that saw approximately 100 activists arrested. They had come for her in the early hours in the Rockey Street, Doornfontein, home she shared with her large family, pulling her out of her bed. A third-generation activist, whose grandparents were involved in the resistance movement, Shanthie's family had gone through the motions of arrests and detentions several times before. In detention she suffered many days and nights of intense interrogation. Now, caught unawares, she was called to the stand. She got to her feet. When Liebenberg instructed her to speak, she looked Judge Bekker on the bench straight in the eye. "I have two friends amongst the accused," she declared. "I don't want to give evidence because I will not live with my conscience if I do." When threatened with further imprisonment, she said: "I am prepared to accept it."[9]

With those three short sentences, uttered in defiance, the foundations of the state's case began to crumble. Over the next few months, more pressure would be put on her to testify, and appeals made to her family to persuade her, to consider her emaciated condition and subsequent detentions that could follow. Her family steadfastly refused to push her onto the side of the government.

Years later, Winnie Mandela wrote:

> It is Shanti Naidoo whom I still see vividly in my mind, her hollow eyes, her thin arms hanging loosely out of that pale ... yellowish, sleeveless dress, her slanted head when she craned her neck in the dock to hear Justice Bekker on that memorable day. When she declared in a firm voice which left no doubt ... How I loved her always, even more now. My admiration and respect for her doubled. Only a person who has been through solitary confinement would realise the amount of sacrifice that lies behind those few words. To my horror, hot tears rolled down my cheeks in the Supreme Court when Shanti said those words.[10]

Nondwe Mankahla, a 33-year-old rabble-rouser from Port Elizabeth (PE), was the state's second witness, but once again Liebenberg was to be stymied. She had agreed to be a witness only in order to stop the beatings during her interrogation at the old Sanlam building in PE – which was to be the venue of Black Consciousness Movement leader Steven Bantu Biko's murder years later – after which she was moved to Pretoria.

On the morning of the trial Nondwe was interrupted during her exercises in her cell and was not even given time to dress for her court appearance – the first time in a year that her comrades, family and friends would see her. "I must have looked like I was coming out of a hole after all those months," she would say later. "I was feeling dizzy in the fresh air."

Despite the months in solitary confinement, and the prospect of further detention or worse, once she was put on the stand she refused to testify. "I do not wish to give evidence against my people" was all she said.[11]

The prosecutor was admonished by the judge, Justice Simon Bekker, who threatened contempt of court charges, to no avail. "What kind of witnesses are these?" he demanded of Liebenberg. But Liebenberg had no answers.

Bekker declared, "I find the accused not guilty. You are dismissed."[12]

At these words cheers rang through the courthouse and reverberated to the supporters outside, who expressed their elation by shouting and singing. Freedom – at last! The elation would last for just a few minutes, however. With barely a moment to feel the sunlight on their pasty skin or to breathe the clean air, the accused were immediately re-detained under the Suppression of Communism Act for a further 90-day period and taken back to their solitary cells. No doubt reprisals for the state witnesses would come. There was some talk that after the Christmas recess, everybody would be discharged, but this did not happen. Each delay was an axe blow. Still, they carried on, fighting the detention with their stubborn refusal to give in.

Relatives of 15 of the 22 triallists tried to obtain court orders to restrain the security police from assaulting or torturing those they were holding for interrogation. An IDAF affidavit tried to argue that witnesses were compromised by their treatment and torture. A British student had fingers prodded in his eyes and was beaten into submission for flimsy information, which included making copies of a document for one of the triallists.

In fact, the security branch had a twofold aim. Apart from detaining the 22 away from the public, to silence them and the more than 100 activists who were arrested in the national crackdown, they aimed to break their spirit of resistance.

Winnie Mandela was then considered the mother of the nation, after the arrest and imprisonment of the male leadership of the ANC. She was a force to be suppressed and silenced, kept away from the masses who edged closer to uprising.

The 90-day detention without trial law was firmly in place. The General Law Amendment Act gave the Justice minister the power to detain anyone under suspicion in solitary confinement without trial for 90 days, and thereafter for further periods of 90 days – again and again, according to a minister of the time, "until this side of eternity." And they did.

A report in London presented by the IDAF said:

> As soon as the 22 accused realised that they had been freed of the charges against them, they began to smile and congratulate one another. Then a loudspeaker ordered the public to leave the courtroom. Police with rifles and submachine guns hustled away the small crowd of people gathered around, while other policemen escorted the 22 into a 5-ton police truck. Instead of being allowed to go free, they were all

back where they had started – in prison, incommunicado, in solitary confinement for a further indefinite period, for further "interrogation" by the Security Police.[13]

Another report from the IDAF, in February 1970, appealed to the world to take notice:

Meanwhile, the imposition of apartheid has become progressively more inhuman, more vicious, more cruel, more intransigent, and literally more murderous. Surely the time has now been reached when the "bridge builders" realise that this activity is valueless and serves only to endorse the policies of apartheid. White South Africans cannot claim, as the Germans under Hitler, that they do not know what is being done in their name. They know, and the overwhelming majority do not heed. And they will continue to close their eyes and to stop their ears so long as the rest of the world accepts them comfortably, so long as it trades with them, plays with them, holidays with them, so long as it too closes its eyes and stops its ears. Everything here is authenticated, and the accounts of torture are taken from sworn legal affidavits.[14]

Also, in February 1970 an editorial in the *New York Times* headlined "Again, South African Justice" referred specifically to the Trial of 22:

In its treatment of 22 blacks charged with working for the banned African National Congress, South Africa seems determined to outdo even its own appalling record for "legal" cruelty and hypocrisy. The prosecution in Pretoria was having deep trouble making a case against the defendants so it abruptly dropped the charges ...

The prosecution was obviously embarrassed by two things: One was the triviality of its own "evidence" against the defendants. The other was the persistence of Justice Simon Bekker, rare in South African courtrooms nowadays, in inquiring into the pretrial treatment of State witnesses, some of whom had also been detained for months under the provisions of the Terrorism Act ... The prosecution's strategy seems clear: It will simply hold the defendants under the Terrorism Act until more "evidence" can be obtained or concocted by the bestial methods that have become a hallmark of South African "justice."[15]

The idea was for the 22 and others to be broken, for their resistance to cease. They would be arrested and rearrested seemingly at the whim of the security police – such flimsy things as love letters and postcards as evidence of terrorism.

The group was interrogated to uncover high-level plots and plans against the government, fed the bare minimum and kept unhealthy, but alive. Sometimes not. The detainees' spirits were low, yet the state feared them enough to keep them under their thumb.

"The freezing loneliness made one wish for death," Joyce testified years later at the TRC hearings. "I keep harping on this, because I do not know if people realise what went on when the Boers wanted to kill peoples' intellect."

The government of the time did not bank on the strength of their convictions.

The trial, *The State versus Ndou and 21 others* of 1969, may not be as widely known as the landmark Rivonia Trial of 1963/64 which saw the leadership of the ANC imprisoned for nearly three decades. The names of the detainees are not as familiar as those of Nelson Mandela, Ahmed Kathrada and others and yet the Trial of 22 changed the course of South African history and the struggle for liberation in its own right. By the "state witnesses" refusing to testify, the case collapsed.

The detainees were eventually released in September 1970, and the slow machinery of the movement continued.

Notes

1 IDAF archive.
2 IDAF archive.
3 Renamed the Internal Security Act in 1976.
4 IDAF archive.
5 IDAF archive.
6 IDAF archive.
7 IDAF archive.
8 IDAF archive.
9 IDAF archive.
10 Madikizela-Mandela, 2013.
11 IDAF archive.
12 IDAF archive.
13 IDAF archive.
14 Collins L. John, 1970, IDAF archive.
15 *New York Times*, 20 February 1970.

4 Joyce Sikhakhane-Rankin

Joyce Sikhakhane-Rankin is probably the most well known among the surviving four women of the Trial of 22. An award-winning author and journalist, she worked at *The World*, *Drum* magazine and the *Rand Daily Mail* at the height of the resistance. Her short book, *Window on Soweto*, published by the International Defence and Aid Fund in 1975, detailed what daily life was like in the township amidst the fights raging against the apartheid government. But it was her recollections at the Truth and Reconciliation Commission (TRC) in 1995 that reveal her most vivid memories of detention, told in fine, grim detail.

Her whole life was steeped in activism. Born Joyce Nomafa Sikhakhane in 1943, she came from a prominent African National Congress (ANC) family. Her grandfather, the Reverend Absolom Mbulawa Sikhakhane, was chaplain of the ANC in Natal. Her mother came from Swazi royalty.

'My parents named me Joyce, and my grandfather added the isiZulu name Nomafa, which means "inheritance". When flattering myself, I am inclined to believe that he named me thus so that I should continue with the political struggle he was involved in with the African National Congress, fighting against white domination,' she says with the playful humour that features often in her writing and her conversation.

Her family moved to Johannesburg when she was a young child. In her book, she wrote:

> I remember as a toddler we dreaded being shunted from house to house because of the shortage of grannies. When there were no grannies available, our mothers were forced to leave us locked alone in a room. They would remove anything dangerous, leaving us with a plate of mealie pap, a mug of water and a chamber pot.[1]

She lived at number 7703 Lembede Street in Orlando West with her parents, Amelia and Jonathan, the latter a lecturer in African languages at the University of the Witwatersrand. The Mandela family lived at number 8115 Ngakane Street, around the corner. "Therefore, during my early childhood

DOI: 10.4324/9781003228905-5

I used to play with the Mandela children (from Nelson Mandela's first wife, Evelyn). The Sisulu family lived a few streets above ours, near the Maketha grocery shop and the Holy Cross Primary School."[2]

When she was seven years old, she attended the Holy Cross Primary School, which was run by the Anglican Church parish of the Reverend Trevor Huddleston, the well-known activist and clergyman. "It was the beginning of apartheid," she says.

> Mum had been a teacher, but she stopped and decided to be a seamstress so she could be with the kids when they got home from school. The person who was a bit ... if I had to find the words ... difficult, was my father. He was a womaniser. He was married but had other women ... side chicks.

She laughs.

In 1954 Bantu Education, the inferior syllabus tailored for children of colour, was introduced. The ANC called for a boycott and the school was closed as a result. For a short while, a home school was held at the Sisulu home, which she attended.

Joyce's involvement in the boycott was part of her initiation into politics, but her grandfather's work also made her aspire to becoming involved. She recalled a time at his home in Clermont, outside Durban, in an interview:

> One event which is always cemented in my mind is the day in 1958 when I helped my grandfather prepare dinner for the Natal ANC members who were in the treason trial, before flying to Pretoria. I shook hands with Chief (Albert) Luthuli, who was then ANC national president, Mr MB Yengwa, Natal ANC secretary, and Dorothy Nyembe, the woman serving fifteen years in gaol in South Africa. They were all so dignified and unperturbed at having to go and face trial which could have cost their lives. They lifted the clenched fist salute and the thumbs-up as they sang *"Nkosi sikekel' iAfrika"* before they left my grandfather's home.[3]

Joyce's high school years were spent in KwaZulu-Natal as a boarder at Inanda Seminary, which was known as a politically leaning institution. She says the impact of this environment shaped her teenage years. "I was also a member of the local (ANC youth group) Pioneers. During the week Grandpa would send me as a messenger to his comrades. I would go to and fro delivering political correspondence and reading materials."

She was at the boarding school when she heard of her grandfather's detention in 1960 during the state of emergency. Her teacher, Edith Yengwa, was also detained but reminded her that "African people would not be intimidated by jails in the fight for freedom."

Joyce and others organised students into the African Students Association (ASA). They would skip school over the weekends to attend political gatherings in central Durban. The ASA was tasked with mobilising the student population against Bantu Education. As a consequence of this, many high school graduates, including Joyce, who were active in politics refused to enrol at the Bantu colleges.

Also, during the state of emergency in 1960, the relationship between her parents ended. As the family troubles ensued, her mother won custody of the children, which meant a return to Johannesburg. Joyce was enrolled in Soweto's Orlando High School, for a taste of the struggle in another epicentre of the movement. There she was introduced to the politics of the Pan-Africanist Congress (PAC), which the students favoured. One classmate was veteran journalist Joe Thloloe.

Her mother was concerned about Joyce handling the separation of her parents. She was sent to the social services office in Fox Street, central Johannesburg, where she met with a social worker, Winnie Madikizela. After her session, during which Winnie interviewed her extensively, it was suggested that Joyce return to boarding school. She was happy, because she was more comfortable at Inanda than in Orlando.

In 1962, after a secret meeting in Durban, addressed by Thabo Mbeki and Ernest Gallo, Joyce was firmly entrenched in the cause. In her final year at school, she won a national essay competition and her teachers encouraged her to pursue journalism as a career. Since she refused to attend "apartheid tribal colleges," Joyce wrote to *The World* newspaper, asking for a job once she matriculated in 1963. They took her on for six months as a cub reporter.

Serendipitously, it was during the Rivonia Trial that she began her professional training, although she doesn't recall covering the trial directly. Instead, she wrote poetically styled articles about the social effects of apartheid. The editor, MT Moerane, was against the anti-apartheid narratives, but Joyce and her former high school friends, Joe Thloloe and Thami Mazwai, did their best to try. Thloloe was detained while working at the paper.

As a journalist with relatively free movement, Joyce was sought out by political activists who knew her or knew of her. She became a messenger between banned comrades, including Albertina Sisulu and Helen Joseph, as well as an "organiser" of secret meetings. Some of these included clandestine forays with Shanthie Naidoo, Rita Ndzanga and other political activists at the toilets in various train stations around Johannesburg.

Joyce again met Winnie, who was by then married to Nelson Mandela, through Rita Ndzanga, who was part of a Soweto cell structure. "Winnie said political things which attracted me. She spoke of the need to resist. She said people shouldn't sit and do nothing because the leadership was in jail."

The cell also included Nkosazana Dlamini (to become Dlamini-Zuma), Mamphela Ramphele and other prominent members of the ANC. As the youngest of the group, the 21-year-old was given the task of gathering young people together, who were then addressed by people like Rita, and elders such as Samson Ndou, who would later be the main accused in the Trial of 22. Joyce was also involved in collecting money for the families of political prisoners via the Anglican Church.

A talented writer, Joyce worked for more than two years at *The World*, then left because of the paper's "thirst for blood" and lack of political direction. She was also put off by the sensationalist slant towards stories about black violence. Although she says "sometimes walking to the train in the morning, one would have to jump over corpses. Crime was very bad at that time and murder rates were high," that was not all that was going on in the lives of black South Africans.

Her parents were momentarily relieved when she left the paper – they did not consider the profession a noble one – more "for drunkards," she laughs. However, the craft wasn't one she could stay away from. She found kindred spirits at the liberal *Rand Daily Mail* soon after the birth of her first child, Nkosinathi, in 1966. Documenting his birth in her book years later, she wrote:

> When my contractions started one of my brothers ran a distance of almost two miles to a local clinic to call a midwife. In Soweto, it is common for mothers to die while giving birth and to give birth to stillborn babies because the midwife and jeep are too late to call. The midwives work under tremendous pressure. Besides those two-to-four-roomed crowded houses are not hygienic as places of delivery, neither are they equipped with emergency units.
>
> The only maternity hospital for African women in the whole of Johannesburg is at Baragwanath (in Soweto). It is reserved for pregnant women who work as domestic servants and who live in the domestic quarters of the white residential areas or in the single-sex hostels. This is done for two reasons, first the apartheid regime would not tolerate the birth of black babies in white areas, although by accident some babies decide to come before time, and thus born at a white man's premises. Secondly, it is done so as to record babies who are not supposed to qualify for the Section 10 permit (which allowed black people to live in white suburbs as servants) because their mothers in the hostels do not qualify, babies who have to be sent to the homelands as soon as their mothers get discharged.[4]

At the *Rand Daily Mail*, she met renowned editor Raymond Louw; she was employed on a contract. Not satisfied with the employment terms, she wrote at the time:

> Because the *Mail* was taking a long time in deciding on my job prospects, I staged a demonstration by walking out and taking a full-time job with the *Post* and *Drum* ... As I was now in great demand, I wanted to prove a point to the *Mail* that as an intelligent black woman journalist, I was a force to be reckoned with.[5]

She proved her point. Louw employed her permanently. She was the first black woman to work on the historic newspaper. Veteran journalists Benjamin Pogrund, Allister Sparks and Anthony Holiday were her colleagues. Because the newsroom was segregated – by law – she was given a whole floor "the township office" and a separate toilet. She shared the facilities with one other person, Jill Chisholm, who later left South Africa to work for a television network in the UK.

In 1968, while working at the *Rand Daily Mail*, Joyce continued to document the narratives of the general African population living under apartheid. While it might have felt normal to some, who accepted the situation as their given lot in life, Joyce saw the atrocities of the systematic oppression. One issue that was close to her heart was forced removals. When people were being removed from their ancestral homes and dumped in far-flung barren areas, Joyce visited those areas and wrote about their experiences. She witnessed a woman giving birth in the open veld in Limehill, an area about 50 km from Ladysmith in KwaZulu-Natal.

Her own experience of poor medical service and that of other women around her encouraged her to seek out allies among the faith community to approach doctors who could offer medical services to the black communities without charge. Priests Ian Thompson and Cosmas Desmond, as well as the theologian and activist Beyers Naude, were among those she approached. The Justice and Peace Commission was formed, a movement of members of the clergy against apartheid. It later became the South African Council of Churches (SACC). With a vehicle and willing doctors, including foreign medical doctors who were in the country as trainees, they travelled around the country caring for those in need. Joyce became engaged to one of the doctors, but the relationship dissolved when he refused to help on the mission. "I threw the engagement ring in his face," she says.

Her weekends were spent with the doctors, recruited from Baragwanath Hospital in Soweto and surrounds. It was there that she met Dr Kenneth Rankin, a Scottish orthopaedic surgeon in training. Just before his internship came to an end and he was due to return to Scotland, he proposed and Joyce accepted. He left South Africa, intending to make arrangements for Joyce to join him. Sadly, it was not to be.

In the early hours of a morning in May 1969, not two weeks after her engagement was sealed, the security branch came for Joyce. Five armed officers stormed into her mother's home in Soweto and arrested her. The move, she believes, had everything to do with her upcoming marriage, which was in contravention of the Immorality Act, which prevented interracial marriage.

She remembers how, on the morning of 12 May, she was woken by security police. She describes this vividly in her testimony at the TRC hearings in 1995:

> They said I was a terrorist, because as an investigative journalist for a Johannesburg morning daily newspaper, I endeavoured to inform the

world about the brutal effects of apartheid on the Black South African communities. After working hours, I had attended to the welfare and educational needs of political prisoners and their families. Both work had been done in the full glare of public scrutiny. Like jackals hunting at daybreak they had to claim a pound of flesh on those of us who were determined to expose the naked brutality of the apartheid system.

Joyce knew that her journalism attracted attention, and that her missionary work collecting funds around the country was considered a crime, but not that it would be as unforgiving as the regime made it out to be. The 2 am wake-up was "rude and unpleasant."

> By pouncing on you in a deep sleep they meant to deprive you of a vital orderly function. They started the anxiety machine immediately and your trauma began at two a.m. As the five Special Branch officers, at gun point, whisked me away at dawn from my mother's house to the solitary cell via the death row cell in Pretoria Central, I was convinced that I would die in their hands leaving my three-year-old, Nkosinathi, an orphan. (She was a single parent at the time.)

It was during the course of interrogation that she learned that the special branch had not only monitored the press, from her inconsequential articles to the more political ones, but they had also monitored letters sent by her to Dr Rankin and others, and vice versa, which included references to their engagement. She considers the act of detention a personal blow against her relationship by the regime.

Another reason for her arrest was that during her "terrorist activity" travelling around the country collecting funds for the families of the politically displaced, she met, briefly, with Nondwe Mankahla in the Eastern Cape. This seemingly insignificant meeting might have sealed their fate together. She knew Winnie Mandela, Ma Rita and Shanthie from the unions. They were all branded terrorists in common.

****

A few weeks after Winnie's funeral, Joyce and I meet for a second time at a Pretoria mall. She was well enough to drive herself in her little Mini Cooper to our first meeting, but today she tells me her artificial knee is giving her trouble. She is dressed in comfortable shoes and a smart blouse and skirt.

We sit at a little coffee shop, watching people go by. She orders a mixed berry smoothie. She can't tolerate gluten, she says. It's anyone's guess what the prison meals would have done to her back then, and she shakes her head at the memory. "Those starchy meals," she says, adding that it is a wonder she didn't develop kwashiorkor from the hard mielies the women were given to eat daily for months on end. We'd already talked about the funeral – she was ambivalent about the proceedings; a lot of history has passed in the decades since she and Winnie were imprisoned.

She has a tic, a hum in her voice, and I wonder if she's aware of it. Whenever she pauses between thoughts, it comes up, a little "hmm." She reminds me to repeat questions, because she has become forgetful. "After detention you continuously … you continuously have that," she points to her temples. "You are never a hundred per cent mentally. Also you have to excuse me because of mental block, one suffers from that."

Joyce's health was deteriorating and a year later, she was unwell and no longer giving interviews, so I was grateful for the sessions we were able to have. Some memories came back easily, and her laugh was frequent and comfortable.

She tells me she felt she was prepared for detention, having studied the journalist and activist Ruth First's memoirs about her political imprisonment in 1963. The comparison was lacking, sadly, because Joyce was an African female whose treatment was far inferior in all aspects. Also, in the short years since Ruth First was detained, her capturers had learned advanced interrogation techniques in France and Algeria. This may sound as if they had had sophisticated espionage training, but these methods were nothing more than prolonged sleep deprivation, intimidation and torture of the physical and mental kind.

She says

Ruth's was the first study which looked into torture by mind-breaking. It won't address the physical torture which we (the 22) went through. In terms of mental health, the very purpose of detention was to wear down the mental capacity of a detainee. You are in solitary confinement. You don't communicate with anyone, not even the wardresses. They just came and brought you the plate of corn, on a plate and bucket (made) of galvanised iron. They would just open the door and put down the dish without saying anything. You were lucky if they greeted you.

This she could have borne, but the separation from her young child was what made her wish for the ordeal to be over. The special branch preyed on this. Years later she wrote:

Being forced to abandon my baby son, Nkosinathi, was untenable torture. To crown it all, during a torturous interrogation session at Compol Building, a three-year-old Afrikaner toddler was brought in to remind me of Nkosinathi. They thought I would break down and accept their communist conspiracy interpretation of what I was involved in.

It is not only your intellect which is important in your life, it is also emotions, your relationships with other people, how to deal with these people. So, when they brought that child they knew how much I was in love with my son. They knew that I would break down immediately. So this is part of the warfare, part of the game. They put the child there. They knew she will crack, she will do what we want and I refused to do that. That is why I am saying, that enduring race which I was in, fighting for change in this country, I think, was a price to pay for the separation with my son. I was not going to break down. So that is another way of the way they dealt with us.[6]

The plot was that Joyce should turn state witness and build the case against Winnie and others who were more deeply involved in the struggle. She never broke.

Despite the agonising presence of a toddler I refused to be chiselled into an instrument of apartheid's evils, intelligence and security design. True, I was longing to be with my son, just to cuddle him, but the price to pay for that was worth our cruel separation. It was worth the strains to gain freedom for all South Africans, but then just opposed with the will to survive, torture by mind-breaking wormed itself within me, enveloping me with feelings of guilt.[7]

Joyce has recorded her story in iterations. But she still frowns, remembering.

It's written about a lot … about how small the cells were, 1.5 metres by 4 metres. I would try to walk to tire myself. If there were insects, you were lucky. There were ants in my cell … you started counting the ants, observing the ants' behaviour and character. I don't remember anything to read. Bibles, sometimes … but they took them away also. I don't remember anything else to read (in nearly two years).

She closes her eyes as she remembers something nasty. "Menstruation, after some time – mine – stopped. It seemed all your body functions were different. I don't know if it was the food." She wrote how women were denied sanitary material, bleeding through their clothes and onto their sisal mats. Three mats were bed, sheet, blanket and pillow – always soiled and never washed.

At the TRC hearings, she said this basic bodily function was used against women to increase their agony:

In detention I was determined to continue to be counted with those who stood for humanity. In the clutches of the Special Branch I had to suffer indignity in order to survive. For example, as a woman you dreaded the commencement of your menstrual period, because it became so public under the notice of your interrogator, who were all Afrikaner males. You had to ask them for sanitary pads.

Winnie Mandela has also written how she was given toilet paper during her cycle, or told to "Go and use your big fat hands." Warders purposely made menstruating women stand as punishment, Joyce says. "The feel and smell of the sticky blood as a reminder of imminent slaughter at the hands of your torturers."

The mind games were meant to wear them down, far worse than the physical conditions. "I just remember the lights were bright, one light hanging down so you can't sleep. You don't know if it is night or day," she says. The thought made her twitch involuntarily.

Their methods were not lost on her. "The first day they brought you in, they made you pass the condemned cell. You saw the gallows and the hanging. Then I was told to strip and go outside. There was a shower outside, and the water was cold," she remembers.

Interrogation was difficult enough, but the mental torture continued in the cell. At the TRC she testified:

> Commissioners, it is very rare that you hear that in Pretoria Central there was a death cell for women. Black women were hung at Pretoria Central. The ghostly solitude of the night would be broken by the hollow clacking sound of galvanised iron chamber pots falling on cement floors. The loudness of that noise would be intermingled by agonising screams of women and babies. Minutes later you would hear gruelling bark of dogs, grunting as if they were tearing someone into pieces. The shuddering noise would gradually die down. You would hear the sjambokking, the hard (sic) rendering scream of the women. This was happening all the time at night.

The human rights violations were endless. Nobody was watching; nobody knew where she was. She was interrogated, tortured, by notorious security branch policemen. They had files on every aspect of her life, including her relationships.

The outside world would have been a step out of the quarantine bubble. The solitude was deafening deprivation. "We were lucky if we saw others. We had to protest to get our rights (to exercise for 30 minutes a day or receive legal counsel) and we still didn't get the time out of the cells. I remember the first time in detention, I was separated from everyone who I thought might be with me. I didn't know of other detainees, except Shanthie," Joyce says. "It wasn't because she was allowed, but she would sing her prayers in the early hours of the morning. I picked up that that's Shanthie. The wardresses were white Afrikaner, we never saw another black person."

She remembers one occasion when she saw comrades between early hearings, and the joy of getting together.

> When we were on trial they would release each of us from the individual cells and put us in Winnie's cell. One time we refused to move away from the cell and the prison warders called in reinforcements. They came in

with Alsatians to force us out. The only thing we could do was strip naked, all of us stripped and then they left us for a while. Otherwise the Alsatians would have attacked and torn our garments. If you were naked they wouldn't be able to bite …

In the many years under apartheid, politically active women were routinely arrested and detained and it was common for young girls to come back pregnant. Joyce was terrified of being gang-raped in the torture seasons.

Then one day she was transferred from Pretoria Central to Nylstroom Prison in Limpopo, about 300 km away. This was where she was pressured to turn state witness.

They offered to release me if I testified against the others. They would change my identification and take me outside South Africa to work elsewhere and be protected. I don't have to harp on the conditions (at Nylstroom Prison). I would protest and demand to know when I was going to be set free, when I would go home. They came one day and took us to Pretoria to be tried. Again we were put in the cell which Winnie occupied. This was a bigger cell and she had a bed, and a cabinet with books. There was a series called the *Angelique* series. Now, these novels are about a French sorcerer who is condemned to death. His wife, called Angelique, wants to save him from the gallows. I picked up one of these books to read and thought it was a brainwash. And then I asked Winnie where she got these. She said: "Oh, they were given to me by the special branch when I demanded something to read". I thought this series was definitely intended to indoctrinate Winnie. I remembered that at Nylstroom they had given me a book called *The Flying Eagles*. You know what happened? After reading that book, I planned to escape. At some stage I even wanted to kill myself. And when I look back now, I think that book was given to me deliberately because at Nylstroom there was no way in which I could have escaped. I would have been shot dead.

Joyce testified at the TRC hearings that, post-1994, criminal behaviour and societal ills might have come directly from the trauma of living under the apartheid regime.

From TRC transcripts in 1995:

26 years have since passed since I was among a group of seven women subjected to torture by mind-breaking by the apartheid Security Police and yet I often find myself back in the dungeons of solitary confinement, ready to take away my life for no explicable reason. This all happens without any conscious thought on my part. I hate it when my mind brings those terrifying memories, but my mind just does it for me. It was orchestrated to destroy me.

She was likely one of the first detainees to write about prolonged mental anguish.

> Today as I move around in the workplace I realise that I am not the only one, I am not alone in my ordeal. Countless of fellow South Africans who survived apartheid incarceration are in constant battle within themselves to continue to live and work. They are on guard, refusing to succumb to the dictates of the mind-breakers who knew the long-term devastation, devastating effects of their psychological warfare against the freedom loving South Africans.

She also believed women who were the wives of political prisoners, detainees themselves and activists, suffered from paranoia and even turned on each other.

> Outside the prison environment family and community relations were destroyed, because the former detainees or prisoners could not cope with a normal family and community life or had been turned monsters against the very cause their lives had been devoted to.

She added that gossip and rumours plagued women in the movement. She herself was subject to this, for years afterwards.

> Between mid-1964 and 1973 I remember that when travelling in trains, buses and at the work place, smear campaigns about the wrongdoings and the plight of the wives of jailed political leaders was rife. We should ask ourselves why is it that such a good person, such a person who was a fighter, why is that person a monster today and we should put the blame where it belongs and we should assist our former Comrades who have fallen. You do not fall just because you die and you are buried. This, the apartheid machinery of torture by mind-breaking was aimed at totally ruining you even if you are alive.

And her prediction, she said in 1995, was that the generation of children whose mothers were heroes, quiet or not, would be worst affected.

> The children were thrown in the streets to fend for themselves. Some swelled the ranks of the liberation movement, the unlucky ones turned tsotsis (criminals).

Rita Ndzanga was one of the many women she thought of when she wrote her statement to the TRC. "Rita Ndzanga, she really suffered, that woman," she says, shaking her head. "She lost her husband, he was tortured to death in detention (in 1977). She was detained and couldn't even attend his funeral. And then two of her sons died, after 1994."

You would never imagine, had you passed this matronly lady shopping at the mall, or browsing in a bookshop, that she had led such an eventful and extraordinary life. Nor that she would make a dramatic escape from South Africa and go into exile. She was denied permission to leave the country and so was instructed by the ANC, and assisted, in 1972, to leave surreptitiously. She would leave behind her six-year-old son, Nkosinathi, and seven-month-old daughter, Nomzamo.

"I got into my political work because of my mum," Joyce tells me.

> Family background counts a lot ... how you were brought up. My mum, Amelia, was very fond of us and she was so loving. Even when she encouraged me to travel for work and (after the trial) to go into exile, when she said she will look after the kids, I could trust her. She was very, very loving.

The ANC wanted Black Consciousness leader Steve Biko to leave with her because they had heard that there was going to be a clampdown. She spoke to Biko. Unfortunately, he refused.

> The first challenge when I had to leave the country was not knowing trust from fiction. The ANC sent a woman, Dolores Godfrey. My mum said: "Why don't you go?" I thought if it is false, I am a dead woman. But you know, seeing you're not able to do anything with yourself as a banned person, I considered it. I'd been a journalist but I was restricted, I couldn't work. I said to this woman, "I need to think about it" but she said we didn't have time and they would come back in a few minutes; that transport has been arranged. That's one of the very difficult decisions I had to take because I wasn't sure what would happen. She said we will go through Swaziland. Suddenly they were taking photos, changing my name. I would be "Sheila", and she gave me a wig and makeup.

Joyce titters at the memory.

She was smuggled to the Swaziland border hidden in a compartment of the petrol tank of a truck. Since the apartheid police had intelligence in Swaziland, she was given a false passport to cross over into Mozambique.

> From there, I realised it was dangerous. There were police all over the place, even in neighbouring countries. From Swaziland we had to drive through Mozambique and then fly from there to Germany. I just said, 'Well, if anything happens, it will happen'. I was 23. You've given yourself to fate and luck.

The pickup van travelled over bumpy roads for a day until she was escorted onto a plane to Frankfurt. There she connected onto another plane to what was then East Berlin.

Arriving in Germany, "The first thing which surprised me was to see white men doing manual work. Carrying dustbins and the like," she chuckles.

ANC leader Moses Mabhida suggested she enrol in a journalism school or go into armed training and conflict with MK. A transcript of an interview with her niece Mbali describes how Joyce started journalism school and she

> recounts a merging of her two worlds, Soweto and Berlin. Once, when scared to have missed her stop with no knowledge of the language, she jumped off the train onto the platform (while it was still moving), as she used to do in her formative years in Soweto. She remembers a man throwing his hat onto the platform to rescue her, presumably out of panic for her safety. She didn't last long at the journalism school because the lecturer "fell in love with her". Given her revolutionary intent, her "mind was not into falling in love", so she asked to leave and told her superiors instead that the schoolwork was repetitive and unrewarding, given that she had already been a journalist for some years. She insisted on joining MK.

Joyce left for Zambia by way of Tanzania. But fate stepped in. In Zambia Joyce lived on a farm with a family who harboured her. She was disguised as a domestic worker and nanny while awaiting her call-up for military training. The farm was a safe house and a stopover for ANC leaders.

By complete coincidence, the Scottish doctor, Ken Rankin, happened to be working as an orthopaedic surgeon at a university in Lusaka. It had been two years since she had released him from the obligation of their engagement, and more than four years since they had seen each other in person. Dr Rankin had heard from his family about her escape, and then about the possibility of her being in Zambia. He tracked her down and with the help of ANC leaders, including Thabo Mbeki, Chris Hani and Simon Makana, tried to get in touch with her. Makana passed on a message to Joyce that Dr Kenneth Rankin was looking for her.

Reluctant to get back into the relationship because of her new military ambitions, Joyce none the less agreed to see him. A meeting was arranged at the farm.

Kenneth immediately reiterated his proposal. After initially being torn between his proposal and military training, she was persuaded by friends to give in to the philosophy of the ANC she came to know: "The struggle is long." They were finally together.

Joyce and Kenneth spent a few years in Zambia, adopting a little boy called Vikela. He was the son of the exiled ANC leader Duma Nokwe, one of the country's first black lawyers and a defendant in the Treason Trial, and Dudu Mate Mfusi (alias Maude Manyosi), who was one of the first females conscripted for the ANC.

It was during this time that she wrote *A Window on Soweto*, over six months, mostly from memory and press clippings. Journalist Ruth First passed the manuscript on to the International Defence and Aid Fund (IDAF), who published it to raise funds for political prisoners and their defence.

In 1974 Kenneth and Joyce left Zambia for Scotland. There she could secure her citizenship and meet her in-laws. And she was pregnant with a son.

While she says she was functional and of sound mind to work and write, she sought psychological help before her children in South Africa came to join her in the UK.

> I started therapy when I was in Scotland. By then, I was known because I was speaking on anti-apartheid platforms as a former journalist and campaigning against apartheid. You feel you have to resist falling into pieces, it's your duty to do that. This was during apartheid times; you can't let the enemy be happy by falling to pieces. Although I would get depressed, especially when the kids hadn't joined me, you can't make the enemy happy. It was a resistance movement. The person who demonstrated that the most was Winnie, you see. She would talk about it … even until just before she died she was saying that we had to keep it up. She really was very strong.

She recalls an isiZulu song that helped keep the exiles' spirits up.

> Sabashiya bazal' ekhaya
> Saphuma sangena kwamany'mazwe
> Laphoku ngazi khonu mama nobaba
> S'landel'inkululelo
> Sabashiy' abafowethu
> Saphuma sangena kwamany'mazwe
> Laphoku ngazi khonu mama nobaba
> Sesithi salan salan'ekhaya
> Saphuma sangena kwamany'mazwe
> Laphoku ngazi khonu mama nobaba
> S'landel'inkululelo
> Nelson Mandela
> Sabela uyabizwe
> Hay Amagerila
> Sabela uyabizwe
> Walter Sisulu
> Sabela uyabizwe
> Thula ntanam
> Silwela isizwe
> Winnie Mandela
> Umama we sizwe
>   *
> We left our parents behind (home)
> We left our parents at home

We are leaving our homes to reach other countries
Unknown to our parents
In pursuit of liberation
Farewell all at home
We are leaving our homes to reach other countries
Unknown to our parents
In pursuit of liberation
Nelson Mandela Respond you are being called
Guerrillas Respond you are being called
Nelson Mandela, Winnie Mandela, Walter Sisulu comforting words
Be peaceful and do not worry my child
We are fighting for this nation
Be peaceful and do not worry my child
We are fighting for this nation.

She says

I didn't see my children for long periods, five years probably. Bob
Hughes, who was a member of parliament in Britain, he handled that
and demanded that the South Africans in exile should be allowed to
have their kids come and join them. If they didn't, he would raise it in
the British parliament that South Africans are holding my kids hostage.
I think because I was involved in the anti-apartheid movement I felt
I was doing meaningful work but it was challenging to be away from
them. You always thought about those at home which are oppressed,
and until they are free, you are not free.

****

Joyce's son Nkosinathi Oliver is a chef in Huddersfield, West Yorkshire, in
the UK. Her daughter Nomzamo lives in Sheffield, South Yorkshire. Joyce
and Kenneth's son, Samora, who was conceived in Zambia but born in Scotland, has followed in his father's footsteps. He is an orthopaedic surgeon and
practises in Newcastle. Their youngest son, Allan, works in 3D technology in
London. Vikela lives in Johannesburg and worked in high-profile corporate
roles before founding a youth education accelerator and learning programme.

Dr Rankin Jr was born shortly after his parents moved back to Edinburgh
to establish his mother's citizenship and create a safe environment for the children. We had connected on social media – again he had mistaken me for a relative of Shanthie Naidoo – and now we spoke of the serendipity on the phone.
It was one of the first occasions he had spoken about his mother's history.

"So I was born in Scotland," he says,

and my younger brother and I had a different upbringing compared to
my three older siblings. My parents made arrangements for Nkosinathi

and Nomzamo to come over. I was very young but I know that when my younger brother Allan was born 1977 we were all together as a family again. I know it was quite an adjustment for my half-sister and brother to come to the UK after living with Gogo in Soweto.

He says he was in awe of his mother and father's "fairy tale love story."

I've always thought it was fate, their relationship. It was quite unlikely how he, a surgeon from Edinburgh, went to South Africa and met Mum. He went to medical school in Edinburg, graduated in 1963 and needed to train as a junior doctor. He was brought up as a Presbyterian and wanted to do evangelical work. But he also always had itchy feet. He worked as a ship doctor and went to Australia. And, he was influenced by the writing of the missionary doctor, Albert Schweitzer, who had worked in Africa and was inspired by that. That is how he ended up at Baragwanath. In fact, he received an OBE some years later, in 2001, for his work in Africa after training many young people, practitioners and medical doctors. It was so progressive of them both, because he did this alongside my mother's contribution as an activist.

He says the family was tight-knit in their time together, perhaps a result of his parents and Joyce's children being separated for several years. "We were always very close, always together as a family. My parents' marriage was so strong, because they had gone through such experiences to be with each other. I've often thought about that dramatic moment when they met again," he says, his emotions clear.

When she was detained, my father didn't think he would see her again, really. And then what were the chances that they would both be in Zambia at the same time? They were in Lusaka and it must have been quite a shock to see each other again, and to get married. And they were happily married from 1974 until Dad passed away in 2011.

He says his mother spoke about the hardships in South Africa, and her and his father's ordeal.

I know their work changed South Africa for the better. Together, they helped to get medical services to people. By helping to recruit people and finding him, they would have impacted many people. Dad's OBE, for instance, was about the work he did to upskill people, sharing with practitioners techniques that were not in the country at the time. You can't measure that.

As for his mother's prison ordeal, Dr Rankin Jr says it had a profound impact on her and the family. "She did speak about the trial and her detention, often. There is a photo with Aunt Shanthie and her, with me as a two-year-old. They obviously met again while both were in exile." Joyce always mentioned the country in glorified terms.

In fact, even when she spoke about detention, although it had a definite emotional impact on her and she was sometimes distressed by it, it was never to the point that she was dysfunctional. It was amazing to me, her having gone through that. It isn't that the trauma she had been through had not affected her, but I think it was largely in a positive way.

The family remained in Scotland until around 1980, then moved to Mozambique for a short while, before living in Zimbabwe for ten years.

"I was fifteen when we flew in from Bulawayo in 1991. It was the first time we were in SA, and the first time for Mum as well. We were met with fanfare!" He laughs, remembering the crowd that greeted the family at the airport. "We stayed in Joe Slovo's house and met Nelson Mandela."

Dr Rankin Jr says he and his brother enjoyed the fruits of their parents' work. However, he isn't sure of the effects on his elder half-siblings who spent about a decade away from their mother. Including her two years in prison, and the seven in exile, Nkosinathi and Nomzamo would have spent their formative years happy with their grandmother.

Mum always said that maybe if they hadn't been without her, it might have been different. But we can never know if things had played out differently. Mum would always say how bad she felt that those things happened and that maybe it did damage them.

When it was time for the children to study, the family chose Glasgow and so they went back to Scotland. Once the children were settled, in 1994 Joyce and Kenneth moved back to South Africa. They lived in Pretoria – close to the Kalafong Hospital where Kenneth worked.

Dr Rankin Jr says:

I had the privilege of flying to South Africa on summer breaks and enjoying staying with Mum and Dad. It was a beautiful time of transformation in the country and they were enjoying it thoroughly. Both were working in government posts. Dad became a professor at Kalafong academic hospital. We were lucky that when I was doing my own training in medicine, we were able to operate together a few times.

Joyce says Kenneth was in love with the continent, as was she. "My husband liked open spaces. We bought a two-hectare plot and initially I was really afraid to be in Pretoria," she says of the then predominantly Afrikaans area. "He said: 'You surprise me because you believe in people. Who's going to hurt you here?' We were fine. There was only one incident when Ken and I were cycling together. We had a tandem bike," she smiles at the memory. "Someone, a neighbour, pulled a pistol from his waist. 'This is why I was afraid', I told Ken." She laughs. "That was the end of riding the tandem. Real right-wingers are dangerous, but the majority of our neighbours are okay. We were happy."

Kenneth Rankin died in 2011, but Joyce continued to live on the small-holding until recently.

Of the women, only Joyce seems to have received formal therapy around her ordeal, which she did in Scotland. "I did go for counselling, because really the best counselling is when you are chatting. It's when you are speaking that you release the tension. The therapist is trained to be empathetic and draw the ill feelings from you. After a session you feel okay, for several days or months. You go again when you feel distressed," she says.

The TRC hearings in 1995 were helpful in debriefing. She gave detailed testimony about her captors, some of whom were granted amnesty, and she says she has forgiven them. "It was the ANC. The message was that the people are not our enemies. It's the regime. The apartheid regime."

When she does have trouble with her memories, she does her breathing exercises. "I've got to do mental exercises. You breathe and you release. I was advised in a therapy, to breathe through them. You allow them to happen. You accept them because they will always be there." She waves her hand in front of her face, eyes closed.

> They're there but one tries not to be bitter because you will be on the path to destruction. What you want to avoid is that they control you, because then you will get mad. You think of something else, other than memories. I find that I have to acknowledge them. There were many who did lose their minds …

On her return from exile she worked for the National Intelligence Agency and the South African Broadcasting Corporation (SABC). She was executive producer of the film *A South African Love Story: Walter & Albertina Sisulu,* and co-producer of *Samora Machel: Son of Africa.*

****

In May 2008, Ruth Muller, an archivist at the Nelson Mandela Foundation, working with Mr Mandela's personal papers, came across a letter, dated January 1971, in a book of family correspondence addressed to "Nomvula."

At the bottom of the hand-written letter (which would have been written out in the book before it was re-written on letter paper and sent – via the Robben Island authorities) was the name and address of the intended recipient:

Miss Joyce Sikhakhane

c/o Nkosikazi Nobandla Mandela

8115 Orlando West

Johannesburg

January 1, 1971 Please see postscript before you read this letter.

> *My dear Nomvula, Re roba matsoho for you & John! Is it true? Can you two really do this to me, take such momentous decisions without even as much as giving me a hint? I must have missed heaps of meat & pudding at the engagement party. To your wedding I would have been accepted just as I am, without having to sport a frock coat, starched shirt & top hat. What is even more important to me, your wedding would have been one occasion in which I could have shined at last. I rehearse daily on a penny whistle; everyone around here calls it that though it cost R2.00.*

> *I'm still on the d.t.l.-stage but with more practice I could have tried Handel's Messiah on it on the great day. You have guts in the proper sense of the term. Was it love, love of adventure or both that made you take such a gamble? There is no insurance house anywhere in the country that could secure you against such an obvious risk.*

> *On as hopeful & as ambitious as John is will most probably not allow the sweet pleasures of an ordered family life to interfere with his pattern of thoughts and doings. Besides, even at a distance, association with a Nomvula would tend to keep him on the ball most of the time.*

> *What do you expect the poor fellow to do when you are actually entrenched right inside his mansion, your ears on the ground and feeling the pulse as usual, now questioning this, condemning that & demanding action all along the line? He will run wild.*

> *They tell the story of a woman (I believe she lives in your street) who has terrific reserves of will-power & initiative, & who made a deal as fatal & remarkably similar to the one you are now contemplating. The going was uphill right from the beginning.*

> *Hardly 4 months after the wedding bells had tolled, some hue & cry on the Reef forced her to live for a fortnight with the matron at Ameshoff St. Yena nowakwakha tight-roped for 48 months when their dreams of a well-organised domestic life abruptly ended. Hubby went & real chaos reigned in her soul & everything around her.*

> *She now lives like a swimmer in a rough sea, battered & tossed about by giant waves & treacherous currents. Is this the miserable life you now wish to lead? I suspect you'll immediately retort by pointing out that on questions of this*

nature I ought to address myself not to you brains but to your breast, persuade not your head but your heart, for it is the latter that John has won; or are you the conqueror? If this be your retort then say I: Hallelujah! Genissimo!! Sermons on such matters, even from well-meaning friends, are out of place. What the heart feels may very often be the sole justification for what we do.

I have known John since the forties & I regard him very highly. He is humane & generous & possesses a lively & sober mind. I sincerely believe in him you've found an ideal partner who will make life for you happy & enjoyable, & who will encourage you to sharpen the abilities that you undoubtedly possess. You've caught a big fish, little sister! Or are you going to prove me wrong once again by saying: Buti, I'm a modest person but I can't help thinking that John is a lucky fellow. It's him, not me, who has caught a big fish. I am the creation's rarest fish, the Coelacanth! This is a duel to be fought between you two, I'll stay out of it.

But I do wish you to know that: Siqhwabizandla! May the wedding day be bright & lovely & the night lit by a golden moon. I should have liked to have written to both of you, but I deliberately avoided such a course. John & I are very close & I can speak frankly to him on personal matters without hurting him. If I spoke directly to him I might be tempted to ignore everything I have said here about delivering sermons.

My letter might both be congratulations & reprimand, (as well as) a demand for explanations which might make conscience itch. But to you I can truly speak as I have done here, & this is how I should like things to be. Remember that both of you are very dear to me. Thanks for the Xmas card sent in Dec. 69. That I never received it makes no difference whatsoever to my sense of gratitude. My only regret is that I was denied the opportunity of possessing a precious souvenir which would have made John & others shrink with jealousy.

It was most kind of you, Thoko, Rita, Miriam & our sister to think of me. Give them my fondest regards.

Have you seen our sister lately? I'm worried over her. I have watched all kinds of storms break loose upon her. The harm occasioned by the ceaseless bombardment to which she has been subjected over a lengthy period is shown by the decline in her health. But it gives me some pleasure to notice that she is taking things well. Give her all my love. You are probably in touch with an old friend I never forget, Benjy. I have wanted to write to him but on every occasion I have hesitated for reasons you would readily appreciate. He is brilliant & fearless, the type of man who must rise to the top of his profession. His dare-devilry reminds me of another friend for whom I had great admiration, Henry Nxumalo, another gogetter.

Give him my greetings. Do you ever hear of Cecil? I once wrote to him but he was already settled in New York when my letter reached the Rand. I'm sorry he had to leave because he played a special role which made him very valuable indeed. In the important media he controlled, he stressed those issues that keep us together as a community. In his office & home he kept a dialogue with those who repeatedly found themselves in disagreement on vital questions & he used his resources to narrow the gaps & to caution against separatism.

Recently I read a stimulating contribution by Lewis Nkosi on cultural problems & I was happy to note that he is still magnificent. My thoughts immediately went back to the mid-fifties, to other friends in the same profession – the late Can Themba, Todd Matshikiza & Nat Nakasa, to Bloke Modisane, Benson Dyantyi, Robert Resha, Arthur Leslie Sehume, Arthur Maimane, Simon Mogapi, Bob Gosani, Harry Mashabalala, Casey Motsisi, Ronnie Manyosi, Layton Plata, Doc Bikitsha, Mayekiso & Ikaneng, all of whom we miss.

Many of them are top chaps & compare very well with their counterparts across the colour line – Ruth First, Stanley Uys, Brian Bunting, Margaret Smith, Charles Bloomberg & others. Needless to say, I did not agree with everything they said, but I patiently listened to them because they often spoke a language I well understood & drew attention to concrete problems. I hope they still try to uphold the high standards. What new faces are there? How is Owen? I have seen a couple of your manuscripts. You'll not feel offended if I tell you that I was highly impressed. One or two lines caused me concern, but my confidence in you helps me to hope that you would certainly be able to give me an explanation which I could accept. Re roba matsoho. With love. Very sincerely, Buti Nel

Miss Joyce Sikhakhane C/o Nkosikazi Nobandla Mandela 8115 Orlando West Johannesburg Postscript: This letter will amuse you. I received information that you were engaged to one of my great friends, hence this note. Though Zami corrected the error, I let it go as originally drafted.

She explains that at one of their secret meeting points, after her release from prison in 1970, Winnie Mandela introduced her to a comrade called Samson "John" Fadana. On seeing her, John immediately professed to have fallen in love.

By then, Joyce had written to Kenneth, freeing him from the engagement obligation two years prior. When "John" proposed marriage two or three days after their meeting, she agreed.

They clandestinely registered a civil marriage at the Johannesburg Magistrate's Court. A day later a carload of security branch officers arrived at her home threatening her with arrest for entering the magistrate's court illegally and being a part of a gathering. The marriage was null and void because it was done illegally.

Joyce said in an interview after the letter was found that she had been in prison for almost two years when she accepted the proposal. "Well, that marriage was never consummated", she laughs.

There were hidden messages between the lines. The "woman in her street, our sister" that he mentions was Winnie Mandela. He shares his pain of her troubles and their brief marriage with Joyce, as a warning about the tough conditions of life under banning orders. Madiba mentions Thoko, and Ma Rita, as well as her journalist colleague, "Benjy", Benjamin Pogrund.

Asked how she felt on receiving this letter 37 years after Mandela had sent it to her from Robben Island, Joyce replied,

> I feel privileged and overwhelmed. At the same time I thank God that through a human act I got Madiba's mind to break from the desolate silence of Robben Island and write such a beautiful, romantic letter. He is an extraordinary soul.

Joyce now lives with her son Vikela in Johannesburg. Sadly, the onset of Parkinson's disease and memory loss has started to affect her daily life. She is yet to finish the manuscript of her autobiography.

Joyce Sikhakhane in February 1972 at Jan Smuts Airport, now OR Tambo International. Picture: *Rand Daily Mail* /Arena Holdings

Joyce Sikhakhane-Rankin, pictured here in 2019, told the Truth and Reconciliation Commission in 1995: 'Today ... I realise that I am not the only one, I am not alone in my ordeal. Countless of fellow South Africans who survived apartheid incarceration are in constant battle within themselves to continue to live and work.' Picture: Phill Magakoe/*Sowetan*

Notes

1 Sikhakhane, 1977.
2 Sikhakhane, 1977.
3 Sikakana, 2018.
4 Sikhakhane, 1977.
5 Sikhakhane, 1997.
6 Sikhakhane, 1997.
7 Sikhakhane, 1997.

5   Shanthie Naidoo

Courage is not the absence of fear, but the triumph over it. The brave man is not he who does not feel afraid, but he who conquers that fear.

Nelson Mandela

The Naidoo children didn't play house. They played "meetings." As a young girl growing up in Doornfontein near Johannesburg's inner city, Shanthie Naidoo and her siblings learned to debate. It was what their family did, even at dinner time. Yes, for fun, Ama Naidoo's children would deliver speeches on a soapbox. As the memoirs about her family are aptly named, resistance was in their blood. Five generations on, the Naidoo family knows little else as their collective life story is wrapped in trials and political warfare of varying degrees.

Shanthie agreed to meet with me once she had rested after Winnie Mandela's funeral proceedings.

The garden of her pretty, yellow, Mexican-style home in Lombardy East, Johannesburg, is clearly lovingly nurtured, and I notice carefully tended plants, herbs and flowers among shady trees. Born on 6 March 1935, she still has a youthful sparkle in her eyes when she opens the door to greet me. She introduces me to her husband, Dominic Tweedie, whom she met while in exile in the UK. She wears a feminine skirt and blouse over her diminutive frame and she stops to apply cerise lipstick before we set off for the nearby tea garden she's selected for our chat. She puts her bag over her wrist and we are ready to go.

The tea garden is a green oasis in a nursery in the east of Johannesburg. Shanthie tells me she retreats here for peaceful walks while adding to her collection of plants. Over scones and tea, she shows photographer Alistair Russell and me the booklet compiled about her family as part of an exhibition at the Apartheid Museum. Her grandparents; her father, Roy; mother, Ama; sister Ramnie; brothers Indres, Murthie and Prema – all of them were activists before any of their actual vocations.

As a child, Murthie would give a speech about how "white people brought us to work on sugar plantations and now they won't let us taste

DOI: 10.4324/9781003228905-6

it". He was five or six. It shows you what kind of home we come from. As a family we would sit together at dinner and talk about issues. The "struggle" is not just the apartheid struggle. This is something the family had been involved in since my grandparents' days – my grandfather worked with Gandhi. And our aunts, parents and siblings were all in the movement.

The history of the family in South Africa starts in the late 1800s. Shanthie's grandparents, Thambi and Veerammal Naidoo, were among the first Indians to join Gandhi's satyagraha movement, which was a form of non-violent resistance meaning "holding onto truth." The aim was to protest and resist unjust laws, fighting for the rights of indentured Indian workers brought to South Africa in the 1860s to labour on sugar plantations. Beneath the headline "Indentured Labourers Arrive in the Colony of Natal," the *Natal Witness* described them thus:

> The ordinary "Coolie" and his family cannot be admitted into close fellowship with us and our families. He is introduced for the same reason as mules might be introduced from Montevideo. He is not one of us, he is in every respect an alien.[1]

"Actually, my grandfather was active in the Tamil community in the Transvaal even before Gandhi arrived," Shanthie recalls.

> At the age of nineteen he petitioned Paul Kruger about human rights abuses of indentured labourers. And then there were women, my grandmother and aunts, who marched across the borders. They went to organise the workers on coal mines and sugar cane fields. The aim was to bring them out of strife. At that time, three people, including my grandmother, were arrested, with the children. So, for my generation, it was not a question of us getting involved, it was *how* to get involved.

Shanthie's grandfather, Thambi, came from a wealthy family. He was born in Mauritius after his parents left South India. A handsome young man – smooth, dark-skinned with strong features – he arrived by ship, landing in Port Elizabeth, and then travelled to Johannesburg to seek his own fortune. He found conditions untenable compared to those on the island that was spared apartheid. He quickly became a leading figure in the large South Indian, Tamil-speaking community in Johannesburg. A devout Hindu, Thambi was greatly influenced by Gandhi's philosophy of satyagraha.

Gandhi described Thambi Naidoo in his book *Satyagraha in South Africa*, published in 1928, as "lion-like," saying:

> He was an ordinary trader. He had practically received no scholastic education whatever. But a wide experience had been his schoolmaster.

He spoke and wrote English very well, although his grammar was not perhaps free from faults. In the same way he has acquired a knowledge of Tamil. He understood and spoke Hindustani fairly well and he had some knowledge of Telugu too, though he did not know the alphabets of these languages ... He had a very keen intelligence and could grasp new subjects very quickly. His ever-ready wit was astonishing. He had never seen India. Yet his love for the homeland knew no bounds. Patriotism ran through his very veins.

His firmness was pictured on his face. He was very strongly built and he possessed tireless energy. He shone equally whether he had to take the chair at meetings and lead them or whether he had to do porter's work. He would not be ashamed of carrying a load on the public roads ... Night and day were the same to him when he set to work. And none was more ready than he to sacrifice his all for the sake of the community ... the name of Thambi Naidoo must ever remain as one of the front rank in the history of *Satyagraha* in South Africa.[2]

Thambi was arrested 14 times for his involvement in various protests. In fact, both Shantie's grandparents were freedom fighters, imprisoned several times in their lives. The women's stories of Shanthie's family are as vibrant, but have been mostly unrecorded. The Naidoo women were relentless, unconstrained by traditional roles. Almost any reference to these women noted how they were known for their political activism as well as their legendary culinary skills. While cooking was and remains a skill, equality and non-racialism was the family ethos, delivered by *seva* – service to humankind.

When miners decided to strike in 1913, the women helped to organise them, and were arrested and sentenced to three months' incarceration in the Pietermaritzburg prison, with hard labour.

"My aunt Seshammal was only a little girl but she marched and protested with her mother, Veerammal, who was heavily pregnant," Shanthie says.

Her grandparents had four sons. One was Shanthie's father, Roy, who went on to study under the poet and Nobel Laureate Rabindranath Tagore at Santiniketan in India, returning to South Africa in 1928. By then he was deeply under the influence of the Indian nationalist movement and the teachings of Tagore, "opening the mind and reawakening the goodness of mankind".

He fell into the steady step of the South African liberation struggle that was gaining momentum. Through politics he made lifelong friends, like the "Afrikaner communists" Bram and Molly Fischer and African National Congress (ANC) leader Walter Sisulu. Shanthie says Roy was an uncompromising believer in the ideals of non-racialism and equality.

The life took a toll, however, and Shanthie's father died in 1953. Her mother, Ama, was a political widow long before his death as Roy was often detained for his role in the Transvaal Indian Congress. She took in sewing to make ends meet and she also rented out rooms to lodgers and housed those in need – including Nelson and Winnie Mandela's daughters, Zindzi and Zenani, who went to a nearby school while their parents were imprisoned.

However, she never stopped her political activities. Part of her daily routine was going door to door, often with a child in tow, to persuade people to join or support various campaigns. She was involved in the establishment of the Congress of the People of 1955 and the compiling of the Freedom Charter. Like Martha Dhlamini and Thoko Mngoma, she was a FEDSAW (Federation of South African Women) stalwart, forming the executive with Philippa Levy, Frances Baard, Sally Ayer, Lillian Ngoyi, Amina Cachalia, Violet Weinberg, Ruth Mompati and Esmé Goldberg.

Ama Naidoo never dissuaded the children from their country's duty. "It was difficult for her to see her children detained and tortured. She used to go from prison to prison looking for us. They were never told where we were, or allowed her to visit. It was not easy, but she gave us all the freedom to participate," Shanthie says.

At the time of Shanthie's arrest, her sister, Ramnie, and her husband, Issy Dinat, an underground activist for the banned South African Communist Party (SACP), had fled to the UK to escape testifying in Bram Fischer's trial. Her brother Indres was serving ten years on Robben Island for detonating a bomb at a railway crossing.

"The home in Doornfontein was an open house … if any of the banned comrades had an interview with the international press, they would meet there," says Shanthie. At any given time Shanthie and her brothers would be banned, living in the same house but, ridiculously, never allowed to be in the same room. She recalls an interview with the BBC, wherein her brothers were interviewed at separate times. "Kuben, Prema's son, entertained the journalist while my brothers took turns to meet him."

Kuben Naidoo, who is now deputy governor of the SA Reserve Bank, was of the next generation in the family; he would be arrested for organising a student demonstration during his matric year and wrote some of his final exams in prison.

The Old Fort and the Women's Gaol in Johannesburg in fact housed three generations of Naidoos. The exhibition about their family at the Apartheid Museum detailed their journey of protest, detention and exile over these generations. It showed how they sacrificed time together, risking life and death in many cases, in the fight for freedom.

Ama died peacefully on Christmas Day in 1993. "Her fervent wish was to see freedom in South Africa and to vote in the first democratic election. She saw freedom, but died a few months before she could vote." Her son Indres reflected: "The hardship my mother suffered all these years, going from one prison to another to visit her sons and daughters. Is there another mother who has seen the inside of more prisons than Ama?"[3]

****

Shanthie lived with her aunt in Marabastad, Pretoria, until she was about 16. She returned to Johannesburg around 1951, and attended the Johannesburg Indian High School for two years. After her father died in 1953, she left school and went to work for a company sewing theatrical outfits for a drama-costume company. But the political work of the family continued and in 1955 she worked as a clerk for the Congress of Democrats, which was allied to the African and Indian Congresses and formed at OR Tambo's suggestion to include other races into the anti-apartheid movement. Her work coincided with the 1956 Treason Trial.

After the Sharpeville massacre in 1960, the Congress of Democrats was shut down during the state of emergency that was imposed on the country, and Shanthie went to work for the South African Congress of Trade Unions (SACTU). She was forced to give up that job after 11 months, around December 1963, when she was slapped with a five-year banning order, which severely constricted her movement. With her brother Indres imprisoned on Robben Island, Shanthie was now the primary breadwinner for the family. She worked part-time at Vanguard Books, a bookstore that was for many decades a trading post for literary leftists in Johannesburg. Other employees included activist Helen Joseph and writer Todd Matshikiza. Of course, ever politically aimed, Shanthie continued her work as a trade unionist and helped distribute contraband material. The family, friends and acquaintances were better defined as comrades. It was a crime for them to associate – because the ANC and its allies to which they belonged were banned.

Shanthie was first arrested on 29 February 1965, on the charge of contravening her banning order. She had gone to court to attend the trial of Bram Fischer. Mohamed Bhana, who had also been banned, greeted her and she held her finger to her lips to warn him. For this, she was charged for "communicating with a banned person" and held in jail overnight. She was acquitted, but on another occasion, when she fell ill and was taken to a hospital, the security police went to her bedside and threatened her for not reporting her "change of address" as required by the banning order.

Shanthie had applied for an exit permit, which was essentially a one-way ticket out of the country. The regime had allowed opponents and troublesome activists to leave South Africa, depriving them of citizenship and prohibiting their return to the country indefinitely. The plan was that she would join her sister, Ramnie, and brother-in-law, Issy Dinat, in London.

Defying banning orders and attending meetings despite the restrictions, she would later learn that her movements were monitored from around 1967. Shanthie and Joyce, Winnie and Rita were involved in various small cells, meetings between both unbanned and banned comrades who would gather to share pamphlets and discuss the state of play for months ahead.

The security branch came for her on 13 June 1969, a few weeks after she had read about Winnie, Ma Rita and Joyce's detention.

I was in bed, at home in Rockey Street. It was a normal day, I was going to go to work at Vanguard. It was Friday the 13th, if I remember. They came in and in front of my mother, said: "Pack your bags, we are detaining you under the Terrorism Act."

"I didn't think I was a terrorist," the petite woman says with a smile.

> Then again, your life is political activism, and I knew that Joyce, Winnie and Rita were detained a month or so before me. It was in the papers. So maybe it was not too much of a surprise. There were informers … we later found out they went to our neighbours … they saw who was coming and going to the house.

She wasn't told why she was being arrested, or given any notice of what was going to happen.

> I packed a few things, grabbed an extra dress or two, underwear. It was winter, I took my overcoat with me luckily … It was so cold on the cement floor. I eventually used it as a pillow. Prema, Murthie and the whole family watched. When the police came, it was not one or two, they would never come on their own. There are quite a few of them … but they didn't do anything to hurt me. My brother asked, "Can she take books?" We found a *Reader's Digest* or two and they said it was okay. When we went to the Old Fort, they took them away.

She was not afraid, but worried about her mother not knowing where she was headed. One could disappear in the cells without contact with the outside world.

"I took a small bag with me, but I never saw it for months. They put me into a single cell, with a jug of water. The cells were so, so cold. We were given buckets (for ablutions). When they found out where I was after a few weeks, the family sent winter underwear, but I never received it," she says.

She closes her eyes and smiles grimly, recalling the gaol, remembering incredulously how people who believed they were doing good were treated so badly. "There were mats … blankets to sleep on." The blankets were grey, rough, often infested with insects, at best tattered and dirty.

Most female political prisoners started off at the women's prison before being moved to larger prisons. The Old Fort was the lesser evil of what was to come.

"I didn't feel as isolated at the Fort. There were lots of women; fruit sellers, people in for (contravening) pass laws; you could hear voices. I was there for two weeks. After that I was taken to Pretoria."

Driven by several security branch officers, she arrived at Pretoria Central Prison, where the façade of the women's section comprised a high rock wall with a single metal door in it. She was put into a single cell. It had a cold concrete floor and was draughty. She didn't know it then, but it would become her home for more than a year.

I was completely isolated. That was really, really difficult to cope with. The family didn't know where I was. I knew my mother would be fretting. I imagined that she would keep going to the prisons around the province, wondering whether I was coming back, you know.

The time alone was endless. They were not informed of any legal procedures or allowed to meet with lawyers. "You're alone and your mind just wanders ... to everything. You think of your whole life. When I ate, I thought of my brother Indres (who was already in prison on Robben Island). He was a vegetarian, but they didn't care. He had to eat to survive. We all did," she says.

Soft porridge for breakfast, pap and sandy vegetables for lunch, sometimes a piece of fatty meat were the special of the day, every day. Undercooked samp, or mielie kernels, also made their appearance under the doors at dinner time, accompanied by a dehydrated supplement, *phuza mandla* (Drink for Energy). Often, the food was left outside and came with bird droppings.

"Solitary confinement is terrible, terrible." Shanthie stresses the point by squeezing the tissue in her hands.

Sometimes I would think, They had better interrogate me. At least there was contact. I didn't have anything to read or anything of the sort. So you exhaust yourself, you do your exercise. You can't sleep, so you want to make yourself really tired. I would march and march. And I would do my prayers in the morning.

She is still a practising Hindu.

Ulagelaam uNarnthu ohthurku ariyavan
Nilavu ulaaviya neermali veyNiyan
Alagil johthiyan ambalatthu aaduvaan
Malar chilambadi vaaltthi vaNanguvaam
Aum, shanti, shanti, shanthi
*
Lord Shiva, the Lord of the world whose grace is a rare privilege to realise,
The unparalleled Lord, who is adorned with the crescent moon
and Mother Ganga in His matted locks,
the Lord whose Light is limitless,
the Lord who has done the dance of creation at Chidambaram.
I pray at your flower-adorned Feet ...
Aum, peace peace peace

This was how Joyce, Nondwe and Ma Rita knew Shanthie was nearby. Joyce had chuckled when she told me: "She would make a noise, Shanthie, singing her prayers early, early in the morning. They (the warders) would tell her to be quiet, but she didn't."

Detained and interrogated for five days straight, tortured by being made to stand on bricks in the interrogation room, in order to solicit intelligence from her, Shanthie suffered disorientation and had hallucinations. The hallucinations were used as evidence of terrorist plots. "During interrogation, I had said something in my confused state ... about flying and gold ... and they took that as evidence," she recalls. "It was nonsense. I had never flown, never left the country, but they were looking for anything they could to imprison us."

When she could no longer bear the strain of standing, Shanthie made a statement, without knowing what they would use it for. "I lost track of time and for periods my mind went blank. I dreamed I was being interrogated. In my dream I was speaking to the interrogation officer."

The dream did not make sense, but after coming to her senses, she had been questioned about it as if it were real. She couldn't discern reality from fantasy. She told them that she had known Winnie Mandela for many years, and Joyce Sikhakhane for a year – "a good friendship" but not much more.

One of the reasons she made a statement in the end, she says, was because the police threatened to arrest her entire family.

When Justice Bekker ruled against Shanthie, he declared: "It is obviously unpleasant to be called upon to give evidence against friends. Your excuse is a moral one but, in my opinion, is not a just one." He sentenced her to two months' further imprisonment and warned her that she would be sentenced again, for a year, if she continued to refuse to give evidence. The judge also sent a message to her lawyer to ask the family to persuade Shanthie to testify as he was reluctant to send her to prison again – it seemed he pitied her because of her emaciated and frail state.

The family rejected the judge's advice. When Murthie shared this with his mother, Ama, she responded: "Whatever Shanthie does, we will stand by and support her."

On 16 February 1970, the attorney-general stopped the prosecution for lack of evidence. There was now no need for evidence from Shanthie as a state witness, and her mother made an urgent application to the court for her release. The security police told the court that they were again detaining Shanthie under the Terrorism Act and that the court could not order her release. Shanthie was not released until June 1970, after 371 days in prison, most of it in solitary confinement, for no offence.

Shanthie says:

> When they sent me home, I couldn't sleep for two nights. And then I couldn't stop talking. I remember ... it was getting over the loneliness. After having nobody to talk to and nobody to say anything to, being cut off. There might have been a war going on outside, you'd never have known. That was the first and only time I took something (medication) to help me sleep.

After a time at home, she decided to leave the country.

> What kind of life was this? I was kept in Johannesburg (by the ban-
> ning order). You couldn't be in the company of more than one person
> at a time. Your friends are banned, who do you communicate with? I'd
> applied to leave the country previously. It was while the British dilly-
> dallied that I was detained.

She could not attend the wedding of her younger brother, Prema, or the funerals of close relatives. She could not talk to her closest friends or travel for
leisure, nor visit Robben Island to see Indres.

Journalist Anthony Holiday wrote in the *Rand Daily Mail* on 16 March
1971:

> So it is back to square one. Shanthie Naidoo goes on with her work in
> a city bookshop and waits for what will happen next. She reports to
> the police every Monday between 7 am and 7 pm. She is careful not to
> attend social gatherings and not to speak to any of her old friends who
> may be banned. She may not publish her feelings in writing, nor com-
> municate them to any newspaper. But the look in her eyes says clearly
> enough: "I am not afraid."

Shanthie applied again for an exit permit to leave South Africa to join
Ramnie in the UK. This time she was relieved to receive it from the minister
of the Interior, in March 1971. But she had further legal wrangles to navigate
first: her banning order restricted her to the magisterial district of Johannesburg and so she needed permission from the minister of Justice to go to
the airport, which was on the outskirts of the city. Permission was refused.
Shanthie remembers the frustration.

> It was quite ridiculous. I had applied for an exit permit and had this
> "permission" to go to England. By law they were not allowed to re-
> fuse you, they had to ... but by banning I was restricted to Joburg so I
> couldn't do anything with the permit.

Pan-Africanist Congress leader Robert Sobukwe faced a similar fate.

> The lawyers who were also handling the Sobukwe case included me
> in that trial, but we lost. Perhaps because of his level of involvement
> and leadership, they heard the case collectively. There was no way they
> would have let a leader of a movement go, but I was not such a threat to
> the government ... or I didn't think so. Eventually, Helen Suzman (the
> only progressive activist in the white National Party-dominated parlia-
> ment) campaigned for me separately, and that's how they finally gave
> me permission.

A big crowd, some 200 friends and family, went to Jan Smuts International Airport in Johannesburg to bid her farewell. They sang *We Shall Overcome*.

"It was strange," Shanthie says,

> because you know you're not going to see your family again for a long time, but not how long or how it was going to be over there. I was lucky my sister was already in England. We also had a few friends in Finchley. In a way, it was like the SA community getting together. We were all anti-apartheid people.

Ramnie had been in London for three years before Shanthie arrived. As a younger sister, away from the country, she felt the anxiety of the family's activities from afar.

On a later occasion I meet her at a Saturday lunch with Shanthie and Dominic, for a revisit of the time in England. "We were always in touch with the family," she says.

> You couldn't just pick up the phone, you had to go to the exchange and book a call, then connect. When we heard she was arrested it was a hell of a shock. My mother was traumatised. Prema and Murthie were home, but banned. Indres was in prison, and I was out of the country. And we had no idea where Shanthie was being held. We had many friends, like Paul and Adelaide Joseph, who had started the Anti-Apartheid Movement in North London where we lived. Because of us being active, we thought we could take up the cause. It was through Labour Party supporters like Denis Healey that we were told she was in Pretoria, maybe three weeks later. They knew nothing in SA, and we had to make representations to find out how she was being treated and so on. Then we found out she was first at the women's prison at the Old Fort before being moved to Pretoria, but as it is with solitary confinement, we had no idea about what was happening there.

Ramnie says that apart from demonstrations to release the 22 triallists, the Anti-Apartheid Movement, which was based in Piccadilly in Central London, wrote about the trial in the organisation's newspaper, *Apartheid News*.

> Each of the boroughs like Cambridge, South London etcetera had a movement, and we were in the Barnett unit in North London with Ben Turok and others. We came together to put a lot of pressure on the UK government to stop the detentions. They took ever so long to give her the exit visa, but for Shanthie to land at Heathrow, we had to get permission for her to be granted refugee status. As a banned person she didn't have a passport and there was no way for her to enter the UK without any papers. We had to petition various MPs, and make representations in the House of Commons to give her political asylum.

She remembers the day the family, including Ramnie's young son and daughter, awaited Shanthie's arrival, which was "really emotional."

> When we got home to Finchley, comrades were waiting to meet her. They had heard about the trial and the torture, and we had, too, although she herself wouldn't speak about it for many months after. But it was a happy time, mostly. People brought flowers and treats, and we had a bit of a celebration.

The reunion was bittersweet, although Shanthie was safe and sound, and freedom of movement in the quaint North London suburb, with its picturesque gardens attached to the houses, wasn't restricted in any way. "We just talked," Ramnie remembers.

> Mostly about the family. While we were away, a few family members, my uncles, for example, had passed away and Shanthie couldn't go to their funerals because of the banning order. But we spoke about them and others at home.

The sisters had not seen each other in four years, and they lived together in London for nearly ten, continuing their work from afar. "The movement was really strong in the UK," says Ramnie. "We lived near a few friends and exiles ... May and Dennis Brutus were friends ... and we would have our meetings and gatherings." Poet, writer and teacher Dennis Brutus had campaigned to have South Africa banned from the Olympic Games of 1964.

There are photos of Shanthie standing outside South Africa House, wearing a warm overcoat, with her long, black hair and dark kohl around her eyes, the same shy smile on her face she gives me now. "We would sit outside and fast for 24 hours," she says, "make a noise until someone listened. It was the end of the Vietnam War, and there were protests, there was the Greek junta, and of course we campaigned for South Africa."

One of the campaigns was an attempt to halt the hanging of the young MK (Mkhonto we Sizwe ("Spear of the Nation")) soldier, Solomon Mahlangu – which failed. A lawyer was dispatched, but his hanging was moved to two hours earlier. "What a waste of life that was," Shanthie says.

Shanthie and Ramnie both worked with the International Defence and Aid Fund. "Actually the place grew on me," Shanthie admits. "It's an internationality about London. We were an active organisation and my specialty was always campaigning for the rights of political prisoners, so we were busy."

Ramnie picks up the story.

> Shanthie was a part of the unit active in staging demonstrations for death row political prisoners. In fact, every weekend was busy with protests for the Anti-Apartheid Movement. Our main aim was to get British

people to take action by boycotting SA sport and imports, like wine, Outspan oranges and Cape apples. We also collected for the school.[4] They needed basic things like toiletries and food, there was no access to sanitary pads and so on.

She remembers one evening, returning from a meeting, they found the house had been ransacked.

> We thought it was a burglary, but there was no forced entry or anything major taken. Every drawer, needlework box, everything … was upturned onto the floor. After some investigations, we worked out it was the BOSS agent.

The South Africa Bureau for State Security (given the acronym BOSS by journalists), which was modelled on MI5, was in charge of national security during the apartheid era. It monitored the exiles closely. "We had people working clandestinely and some came to stay with Issy and I at the house in Walmington Fold. We didn't realise how closely this was watched," explains Ramnie. "After 1994, when Mac Maharaj was searching for his files at police headquarters in SA, he found some of ours. Then we learned that our homes, telegrams, telephone calls, everything was intercepted."

It was not all politics and organising in London, and the news from South Africa kept the family in close contact.

> We were quite social as a community and Shanthie enjoyed it. But there were also lots of times when we got messages someone had died, and it was just the two of us to mourn. Of course, my brother Prema was arrested, then Murthie. It was always very emotional and we had to support my mother in SA from far away. Once, when my mother was visiting in London, we heard that Prema's son Kuben was arrested for arranging a march. He was very young, a teenager. My mother took that really badly. We didn't know where he was, and again they phoned us in London to try to find out. We had to write to Margaret Thatcher, and she actually did find out where he was being held and wrote back to us. This was all during his matric exams, and he wrote one or two subjects in prison.

Shanthie was among the delegation who attended the 1973 World Festival of Youth and Students in Berlin. This was a global youth solidarity organisation for democracy and against war and imperialism. She was also elected to attend the Komsomol Party school in the then Soviet Union; she lived in Moscow for a year and learned much about the revolution.

She met Dominic Tweedie, a reporter for the *Morning Star*, on a boat trip to Calais organised for activists. I remembered my first meeting with Shanthie in the tea garden east of Joburg. Before we left, Dominic had said to me: "Take care of Shanthie," his English accent still there, but faint after 20 years in South Africa.

"I was born in Devon, but my family lived between Mombasa in Kenya and the UK," he tells me now.

> When Shanthie and I met I was back living in London with a South African exile family, the Nannans, in East Finchley and working for the *Morning Star*. Shanthie was living at Ramnie's house in North Finchley, not very far away. But we did not actually meet until we all went on the day-trip across the English Channel to Calais, organised by the *Morning Star*.

With a twinkle in his piercing blue eyes, he adds. "So we met in France."

The love story blossomed. Dominic was enchanted by the spirit in the young woman who was so determined to see her country's freedom, even from across continents. He became a freedom fighter for South Africa too.

> Most of the ANC comrades in London kept in touch with each other. They were a "community" of sorts. They had a lot of friends in the Communist Party of Great Britain (CPGB), a connection that went back to the 1950s, at least. Of course, we are political people, and we met in political times, and within a community of political people based in London: Communists and South African exiles. Of course, Shanthie is a "hardliner". She has a very strong grasp of the political basics, and she sticks to those basics. We were part of a number of people who were all part of this huge story and Shanthie was familiar with many of them.

Dominic and Shanthie married in Tanzania when they were working at the ANC's school in Mazimbu. The school's purpose was to give the youth who had fled South Africa after the 1976 Soweto uprising and the children of activists already in exile a primary and secondary education. For some, it was an opportunity for an alternative to the Bantu Education they would have received at home. It taught both an academic and a vocational education, existing off donations and sustenance farming.

Dominic taught carpentry and woodwork, along with hardline political ideals. He is self-deprecating about his contribution – "I am inconsequential in this story" – a sentiment with which Shanthie, of course, disagrees greatly.

****

Despite being away from South Africa, Shanthie Naidoo's bravery was remembered by many in the movement. A political drama, *Shanti*, was written by playwright Mthuli ka Shezi in 1971. Through his writing and his plays, Shezi introduced scores of South Africans to Black Consciousness ideas. In 1972, he was brutally killed – pushed in front of a moving train at the Germiston railway station when he went to the defence of African women who were being drenched with a hosepipe by a white station cleaner. The play was then performed by the People's Experimental Theatre in Soweto and by a drama group called Shiqomo (meaning spear) around 1973. Although fictional, *Shanti* was an ode to Shanthie's beliefs in both the ANC and the Black Consciousness Movement. A political theatre being in possession of the script was also used as evidence of treason by other detainees.

The play was performed in Soweto and Lenasia, and then in KwaZulu-Natal by the Black Consciousness theatre group TECON, telling the story of an illicit inter-racial relationship between Thabo and Shanti, with the aim of fostering unity amongst broadly black communities.

"Shanthie was quite famous then, wasn't she?" Dominic jokes.

> But the idea of the play was an effort to unite African, Indian and Coloured people, and it was historic in this way, because it dealt with the many crossovers of influence between the ANC and the Black Consciousness movements. Both the imaginary Shanti and our Shanthie symbolised this effort.

In the early 1990s the exiles began a staggered process of returning home to South Africa. Of the couple Shanthie came home first, then Dominic a year or so later. Shanthie was instrumental in the re-establishment of the ANC Women's League. She says she was fortunate to find work at Wits University, in the Education Policy unit. "It was part of the work I was doing in England. Dominic joined COSATU, where he spent many years as secretary."

But integration was not easy, even at the family level, after 25 years away. "Coming back was difficult," Shanthie admits.

> When I left, our family was living in Doornfontein. When we returned, they were in Lenasia (following relocations in accordance with the Group Areas Act). There were brothers getting married, and new sisters-in-law, nephews and nieces who were grown up. To build relationships again was difficult. We felt we were imposing, overcrowding people, before we found our home. Also, we had the freedom of movement in England ... travelling by train at night and so on, that we still don't have in South Africa. You felt a little restricted.

Nevertheless, they were happy to be in a country that had survived the long years of struggle, and to which Shanthie had contributed greatly. She was home to see the last days of her mother and one of her brothers, Indres. Indres passed away in 2016.

Their time now is spent in peace, restful at the yellow house. Shanthie is an accomplished cook and gardener. She and Dominic didn't have any children of her own – Shanthie says she married too late in life – but she is proud of her grandnieces and -nephews, whose photographs are displayed on the polished wood furniture.

Although her night terrors haven't left her, a reminder of her time in solitary – "Even now, I don't like to be alone if Dominic has to be somewhere" – life did move on.

Dominic describes her as a pillar of strength. "Not only for me but over the years, as comrades went different ways, it was going to be very lonely without Shanthie. I cannot imagine that my life would have been worth much, without her." He says he can't articulate the connection between them, which brought him to Shanthie and South Africa with it.

> Shanthie and my marriage goes back to more than 40 years ago. I have to inform you that love is madness and mystery. It is impossible to explain. I am still surprised and grateful every day for the love of this wonderful woman. She is a very special kind of person. She has a capacity for open wonder and delight in the natural things, and the human things of this world. It's something rare. Being with Shanthie can be pure joy in any place or at any time. It's fun to be with her. I love her.

He remains in awe of her contribution and the work she and others did, claiming that it takes a special human being to choose a movement when it is much easier to stand by and do nothing. "As I look around I realise that Shanthie is a beacon for a lot of people. I think they see in her, what I see in her. Shanthie is a leader, for sure."

Despite her difficulties in life, in her 80s Shanthie is strong and able, the only sign of her age a slight loss of hearing. Her spirit is as strong as ever. She seemingly handled her detention and exile with grace. Living to see freedom, however problematic it may be today, she says, was worth her contribution. Their work, even as retirees, educating young people in various ways, not least Dominic's treasure trove of Communist teachings, which he shares via social media, is ongoing. They attend gatherings of old comrades, parties and funerals. Family gatherings are still centres of robust political discourse.

Shanthie is of the opinion that "democracy is an ongoing development." She recalls joining a neighbourhood pottery class and meeting women her age who knew little about the struggle against apartheid. It was as if they'd missed that time completely. "I was quite disappointed, but we knew there was a lot of work to be done to rebuild." She gives a wry smile. "It is still not quite done."

Shanthie Naidoo in June 1971. Picture: Arena Holdings

'Solitary confinement is terrible, terrible,' Shanthie Naidoo told the author in 2019. 'Sometimes I would think, They had better interrogate me. At least there was contact. I didn't have anything to read or anything of the sort. So you exhaust your-self, you do your exercise. You can't sleep, so you want to make yourself really tired. I would march and march.' Picture: Alaister Russell/*Sunday Times*

Notes

1 *The Natal Witness*, 8 January 1875.
2 Gandhi, 1928.
3 Naidoo, 2016.
4 The Solomon Mahlangu Freedom College, an educational institution that had been established in Mazimbu, Tanzania, in 1978 for the children of those in exile and young MK recruits.

6 Rita Ndzanga

The main road in Senoane, Soweto, teems with cars and taxis, children going home from school and wandering dogs interspersed with street sellers.
Anyone you ask can point out the home where Ma Rita, as she is known,
lives. Into her 80s the retired parliamentarian, who served under three pres-
idents, was still attending veterans' meetings and getting involved in community projects but she has slowed down in recent years. At 85, the age she
is when she agrees to have a brief meeting with me – she guards her time
fiercely – she might look frail but there is fire and fight inside her.

Rita Alice Ndzanga was born on 17 October 1933, the third child of Isaac
and Alina More. They were farmers, establishing a village called Mogopa
near Ventersdorp in the Transvaal. The community Rita was born into, the
Bakwena ba Mogopa, had been evicted from their ancestral lands in 1912.
Rita recalled in an interview with the Ahmed Kathrada Foundation: "According to my father, my grandfather and others came together when they
were being ill-treated and chased away by the Afrikaners, and bought two
farms which they called Mogopa."

The first wounds of apartheid were inflicted on her as a young girl, and
they sparked her political awareness. The family moved to the vibrant
multi-cultural area of Johannesburg called Sophiatown, where her father
worked as a laundry delivery man. Her mother returned to the village from
time to time, but the children stayed in the city for easy access to school.
And they enjoyed the dynamic melting pot that was Sophiatown. The suburb was home to artists and creatives, musicians like Miriam Makeba, Hugh
Masekela and Caiphus Semenya. Writers like Can Themba, Es'kia Mphahl-
ele, Nat Nakasa and others were drawn to the energy of the community.
That the community celebrated the Chinese New Year, the Hindu festival
of Diwali, Christmas and many more festive occasions indicated the span of
the spectrum of its residents' lives.

The More family attended the nearby Anglican church where community
leader and activist Trevor Huddleston was the parish priest, and tastes of
rebellion would have been delivered with sermons. In many ways the area

DOI: 10.4324/9781003228905-7

was an idyllic one – but that was not going to be allowed to thrive by the separatist government.

> We were still staying in Sophiatown when there was a little bit of talk about moving. You know, after the National Party got into power, Dr Verwoerd was visiting in Sophiatown, and we all wondered why. After his visit, there was this talk about Sophiatown being a black spot and that we were going to be moved. But that took about two to three years because first they had to build those long houses in Meadowlands.

In 1955, 2,000 policemen, armed with handguns, rifles and knobkerries, moved into Sophiatown and forcefully began to separate its residents and move them to different areas, in accordance with the Group Areas Act.

"I was about 23. When the removals occurred, the people of Sophiatown didn't want to go. We didn't want to go. People protested," Ma Rita says.

But over the next eight years, Sophiatown was flattened and wiped off the Johannesburg cartography, later to become the white Afrikaans suburb of Triomf.

The African families were relocated to Meadowlands; coloured and Indian families were moved to Eldorado Park and Lenasia, respectively, both of which were in the dusty south of Johannesburg; Chinese families moved to central Johannesburg.

> They removed my father and my two brothers from our house in Sophiatown. But my father didn't take a house in Meadowlands. He was working at a place called Rand Steam Laundries in Auckland Park. They put him in Meadowlands Hostel, where he stayed with my younger brother. My eldest brother, Matthews, went to Botswana to teach. My other brother, Peter, got his own house ... with a *mkhukhu* (shack), in Naledi. The destruction of Sophiatown split my family up. It was painful.

Ma Rita's journey into politics was natural, after the feisty young woman felt the effects of segregation at all levels of her upbringing. But her activism was cemented when she started work as an administrator/secretary at the Brick and Tile Workers' Union. Part of her work was to be responsible for collecting members' subscriptions. "I didn't even know what a union was," she says. "I just went in because they gave me a job that was paying me something. That's where I started learning about unions."

But she soon learned. Working with unions throws a person into the political sphere at the grassroots level, she maintains, to the workforce worst affected by the systems of government. And so her decades-long dedication began, fighting for the rights of the African workers who underpinned the South African economy.

The union was dynamic and among her friends, who would later be her fellow triallists, were leaders Samson Ndou and Samuel Solomons Pholotho.

Members of the executive were Leon Levy, John Nkadimeng, Mark Shope and Billy Nair.

After a year, Rita moved on to the Railway and Harbours Workers' Union where she documented workers' complaints.

> Most of the cases at the railway had to do with injuries, because they didn't have machines to carry rails. I don't think you ever saw the way they worked. There would be two long rows of singing people, working in a rhythm ... clamp on the rail this side, and swing to that side. But sometimes people get clumsy, somebody makes a mistake and then the rail drops and breaks a man's leg. And most of them were not paid when they were injured. No such thing as proper compensation. Most of the cases I handled were workmen's compensation cases to claim for injuries ... It was not much. Some of them were permanently disabled, because they had to have their leg amputated and couldn't work again.

She remembers that the employers, the South African Railways and Harbours, found the unions a nuisance. They were not allowed to rent premises and had to surreptitiously sign lease agreements using use false documents. If they were found out, they were evicted.

It was here that Rita met her husband, Lawrence, a tall stately young man with a high forehead, who worked as a recruitment officer and an organiser for the African National Congress (ANC).

Lawrence was actively involved in recruiting members for the union around the country. She remembers that he often dressed as a railway worker to mingle with the workers. And, Rita says, he often had to flee from sites when discovered. There were many escapades and close shaves.

> My husband used to go all over the country to recruit, and then try and set up local offices. One time he went to Bloemfontein. He was disguised in brown railway overalls but he forgot to take off his tie. He was talking to the workers as if he was one of them. And then somebody noticed the tie and reported him.

The workers saw the police coming and quickly bundled him into a goods train, but he was spotted.

> And the spies said, *"Daardie een met die rooi das!"* (That one with the red tie) so he had to get off and run. There were houses next to the station and somebody from one of these took him by car to the next station to get a train there to come back home.

It was by no means an easy time. "We were organising under pressure and we were being harassed," Ma Rita tells me, "and we could be arrested any time for organising a trade union because they said it was all about the ANC (which was banned)."

Rita and Lawrence married and moved to Soweto. It was at this time that she met Shanthie Naidoo and her brothers, who were also involved in mobilising unions. Joyce Sikhakhane and Winnie Mandela, also activist residents in Soweto, were friends, as Lawrence and Rita were involved in setting up the local ANC branch in Senoane.

In an interview with the Ahmed Kathrada Foundation, Ma Rita describes how she met others who were part of the Trial of 22.

> You know, after the ANC was outlawed, there were instructions that we must organise ourselves into small cells of not more than four people. But we sometimes came together to get instructions. Winnie Mandela was leading the groups and a man called Ntate Motau from Dube. In my cell we used to come together to make pamphlets and distribute them.[1]

Both Rita and Lawrence were banned persons (since 1964) and as such the couple was monitored closely. They were obvious targets for the raids in May 1969. The Ndzangas were among over 100 people who were arrested between May and June that year.

Ma Rita's home today is renovated and comfortable. "When we got here it was veld, there was nothing," she says.

> Then he (Lawrence) got a truck and brought me corrugated-iron. We made a little shack and we slept there. Then the next day there was a bigger shack. That is where my second child was born. There was not even a toilet, let me tell you. Ma Tshababala was down the road, I ran to that place to relieve myself. She said, "Here if you want a toilet, take your receipt and go to the municipal office and go get a bucket." The lives we led! Really, man, we suffered. I had to work. How much was I, as a black person, earning at that time?

She shrugs. "Nothing, next to nothing. We survived, and we built the house."
She points with a frail finger to a photograph in her lounge.

> There is my father. You see that old man with the hat on? That is the only photo we have in this house … this one. They took all our photos, the security police. A lot of our people lost their things …

Despite their banning orders the couple continued to recruit young people to leave the country for exile, and to travel to training camps around Africa. They also continued with one of the only forms of mass communication of the time – reproducing ANC leaflets sharing news and directives of the movement.

The couple and their young family knew no peace.
Rita remembers the time well.

> News travelled very fast. The government knew we were involved with
> the trade unions, and the activities we were organising. Once you go
> into politics, you can't go out. In the evening people would gather here
> after work. We would talk to people and they would put in their reg-
> istration to be members of the union or the party. When the security
> police came to your house and started harassing you, you know the next
> thing will be detention.

Rita and Joyce had in early 1960 visited ANC elders Albertina Sisulu and
Lillian Ngoyi to deliver a message from Winnie Mandela about joining an
underground initiative. MaSisulu warned the "two young ladies" about
their gathering. She and Joyce should conduct their activities separately,
she advised, because they were both banned. The security police would
pounce on the smallest bit of evidence that they were working together.
While MaSisulu was fond of Joyce and Rita, she felt too many people knew
about their activities. She knew that, like herself, Winnie was a major target
for security police infiltration. In their situation, caution and patience were
essential and she expressed to the women that she did not believe that these
were Winnie's strong points.

Sisulu warned the two not to take unnecessary risks but according to
Joyce: "Young radical activists that we were, we did not heed MaSisulu's
words." Lillian Ngoyi was much moreblunt. "You, Joyce, when the security
police give you electric shocks on your genitals, what will you do? Can you
guarantee you will not talk?"

In the early hours of 12 May 1969, Rita and Lawrence were forced awake
by banging on their doors and windows. With the police dogs, large Alsatians with gnashing teeth, and bright flashing lights through windows, the
children were roused from sleep. The police proceeded, over several hours,
to search the house with little regard for the terrified screams of the four
Ndzanga children. In the end, they confiscated books, private letters, newspaper cuttings, and photos which had nothing to do with politics, or, if they
were political, were not illegal. None of these items was ever returned. At
the end of the search, Rita and Lawrence were taken to the Pretoria Central
Prison.

It wasn't the first time they had been picked up. "I think on three or four
occasions, myself and my husband had to leave small children here in the
house, and did anyone think of my children, these children at that time?
They did not." Leaving her children behind was what worried Ma Rita most.

The couple was taken into detention and would remain in solitary confinement with no news from or about their children. Although the children
were in safe hands later in the day, the image of them being left behind in
the early hours of the morning haunted Ma Rita throughout detention, in

nightmares and visions during interrogation. She recalls that specific moment in time even today as her memory chooses where to take her.

Because the identity of detainees was kept secret from their families and friends, neighbours would suddenly notice the house was quiet. For their relatives, it was not feasible to search for them at the various prisons. They were untraceable unless word got out by chance. Kept in solitary, Rita and Lawrence wouldn't have known where the other was or if one had been released. There was little jurisdiction over the application of the Terrorism Act in any case.

Ma Rita was to remain in prison for six months before the court appearance in December. "When I left home, I left only with my skirt and the coat I had on, and a beret. I had nothing else. I stayed in prison for six months without any change of clothes." The ANC-appointed lawyers brought her personal items when they worked out where their clients were. Closer to their second trial dates, they were allowed consultations. By then, little could be done as the detention orders had been renewed for another year.

Sitting at her dining room table today, she uses her hands to show me how young her children were when the couple were arrested. "Our kids, three boys and one girl. They were small children," she emphasises.

> Those apartheid police had no fear, no shame to take the father and mother, and leave small children like that. My sister had to come and stay with them (when she heard about the arrests, later in the day) but I didn't know.

She wasn't told who was with her children, and for months lived with the guilt that she had left them alone at home that morning.

"What could they do, when police take their father and mother? As a mother, you will cry, cry ... like any mother would feel when they leave small children at home without anyone taking care of them," she says.

****

Four days after her arrest, the security police began their interrogation of Rita. She was viewed as a long-serving activist, organiser and leader, and the security branch was particularly brutal towards her.

> In the interrogation room, they ordered me to take off my shoes and stand on three bricks. I refused to stand on the bricks. Then one of the white security police climbed on a chair and pulled me by my hair, and dropped me on the bricks.

He stopped to wash her hair from his hands.

They again asked her to stand on the bricks. "I fell down and hit a gas pipe. The same man pulled me up by my hair again, jerked me, and I again fell on the metal gas pipe," she says. She might have fractured her arm, but received no treatment for it.

Months of nothingness passed.

On 1 December 1969, Rita was fetched from her cell and put into a van with four other women. When she enquired what was going on, it was Winnie Mandela, who responded, "They are going to charge us, Rita."

Rita's aunt and sister were among the crowd outside the Old Synagogue and they hurriedly informed her that they were caring for her family. After eight months of silence, her nightmares were slightly muted.

In the trial, the police testified that in the home of the Ndzangas, they had found press cuttings on the lack of school facilities for African children and a photograph of Lawrence Ndzanga giving the "amandla" salute.

The state called over 20 witnesses to testify against the defendants. A report from the time recorded:

> Damning evidence was given by a Simon Skosana. He had over a period of time transported activists in the Soweto area to and from meetings. He had been assistant librarian at the United States Information Service (USIS) in Johannesburg and testified to having attended meetings with five of the accused. Winnie Mandela, helped by Joyce and Rita, had duplicated a leaflet at the USIS offices one Sunday in March 1968.[2]

Fifty years on, the pain is still fresh and Ma Rita's mind goes back to the days, and always to the plight of her children. She repeats: "I left small children, my babies. Nobody cared about them. Not even the Anglican church came here. I'm telling you, it was hard."

The spurious charges were obvious even to them as laypeople.

> Our lawyers made sure they separated the charges. We didn't know how to use guns, so they couldn't put us together with others, like one who they said was a guerrilla (Samson Ndou, the first accused). Then when they said we are dismissed, we thought we were going home.

But they were not going home.

"They detained us again. We didn't even go to get our bags (sent by the family). They said somebody will bring them to us, but they didn't for a long time. That was the life we were used to in this country," she says.

Joyce was the one who told me that Ma Rita suffered the most, if there was a scale to compare. No doubt, she was beaten viciously by interrogators for her activities.

"I was in my 30s then, but I can feel it now," Ma Rita says.

> If I move, I've got pains. I am ill from that. In jail, there were doctors that they would take you to see if you were sick, but we were scared to take what they gave us. Anyway, what can you do with a Panado? Those

matrons would give you your tablets when they want to. We got sick. I had high blood pressure. When you are in detention you stay alone, the whole day, and you sleep. If you do get sick, nobody knows. And you wake up again, she says.

Some prisoners were on chronic medication, but it was not administered regularly. "They give you a tablet when they feel like. If they are off work you won't get a tablet. They didn't care, and they did what they like."

Her mind wanders again, back to the interrogation sessions. "You know, I fell on bricks. Those bricks which were set there on purpose. Even now, I have pains."

After 491 days of detention, the Ndzangas were placed under house arrest and each was served with a five-year banning order. They could not leave the magisterial district of Johannesburg, nor attend any political gatherings or meetings. They were not allowed to meet with any other banned person. They certainly could not continue to work for the unions. Rita recalls,

> They planted spies all over, even in my house. Neighbours were given phone numbers so that when they see any car near my house they must take the number. But the neighbour would come back and tell me about it.

Their work in the movement did not go unnoticed. Albertina Sisulu expressed her concerns when the news of the 22 and their torture experience came out. Using Winnie's clan name, she wrote: "Ngutyana and friends are still away and that is not treating us well at all." ANC leader Walter Sisulu managed to smuggle a letter of encouragement to Rita from Robben Island, and she responded on 20 October 1970:

> I was so happy to receive a letter from my leader. It is such an honour to both me and my husband. We never knew we meant so much to you. We are out, as you already know. We are waiting for the results of the appeal lodged by the prosecution. We already know what to expect.

Lawrence found work at a laundry in Johannesburg. He would travel on a bicycle, collecting and delivering laundry. Rita worked at a furniture shop called Porters, in Kliptown, Soweto.

Despite the banning orders, they continued their work organising, recruiting union and party members and assisting young people to escape into exile.

In 1976, Lawrence and Rita, along with a young Soweto activist called Kehla Shubane, were again detained in a police raid, this time at the Old Fort. During an interrogation session, Rita and Lawrence were both taken, separately, to the Johannesburg police headquarters at John Vorster Square, which was known by then for detainees' "suicides" from the top floors. Rita remembers being made to walk barefoot up and down Nugget Street in central Johannesburg, being questioned for hours while sleep deprived. At some stage, a warder approached her to ask, "Are you not Lawrence's wife?" Rita confirmed that she was and the warder walked away. About an hour later, another warder came to her and informed her that her husband had died.

Lawrence is among 166 people who died in apartheid's jails.

The police claimed that the stress of being detained and interrogated – and tortured, Ma Rita believes – led to her husband's fatal heart attack on 8 January 1977.

Rita was not allowed to attend Lawrence's funeral. She pleaded with her captors to release her, but was only allowed to leave the day after his funeral.

> When I was released from prison, my only thought was to go to the grave of my husband. My lawyer, Ismail Ayob, informed me that he had been told to take me to Winnie's house. I was not happy to stop anywhere, but I went. When we got to her house, Winnie called and said, "Rita, I know you want to go to the graveyard but you cannot go in the clothes you wore in prison. Here, please, take my black dress."

In that year, 1977, Ma Rita and her family received several blows. In just a few months, she was alone at the Senoane house. Her eldest child, Andile John, left for exile, and a short time after the death of Lawrence, their second child, Jongizizwe Ezekial, also left the country, for Tanzania. He was followed by Rita's remaining children, her daughter, Nomathamsanqa "Thami," and her youngest, Cecil, who went to Tanzania and then Germany to study.

She returned to work at Porters in Kliptown, always under strict surveillance.

Despite the restrictions, she continued to contribute to the new, more militant culture emerging in Soweto. She was among those who influenced and mentored the "young lions" of the ANC Youth League. Part of her continuing work was to encourage the gathering and administering of the movement and the formation of many women's groups. In the early 1980s, her banning orders finally lapsed. Rita left Porters and returned to the trade union movement.

On 20 August 1983, Rita was among the 10,000 people who attended the launch of the United Democratic Front (UDF), which was held in a community hall in Rocklands, Mitchells Plain, in Cape Town. The UDF incorporated about 400 civic, church, students', workers' and other organisations across all lines of race and gender. The umbrella movement's goal was to establish a "non-racial, united South Africa in which segregation is abolished and in which society is freed from institutional and systematic racism."

In addition, she dedicated her time to reinstituting the Federation of Transvaal Women (FEDTRAW) in December 1984, bringing together women from around the Transvaal. Its second iteration was multiracial.

Sister Bernard Ncube was elected as the first president of the federation, while Albertina Sisulu, Rita, Francis Baard and Maniben Sita were elected as active patrons.

In the late 1980s, the German Anti-Apartheid Movement extended an invitation to Congress of South African Trade Unions (COSATU) to visit the country, and Rita was part of the delegation that visited. After nearly a decade, she was reunited with her daughter, Thami, and son Cecil in Berlin. Thami and Cecil studied in the city. On the return trip to South Africa, she stopped in Tanzania to see her sons, Andile and Jongizizwe, who were training at the MK (uMkhonto we Sizwe ("Spear of the Nation")) school. It was the last time she saw Jongizizwe before she received news that he had died. "They say he had meningitis but I don't know. He was away from me for so long," she says. His remains were exhumed and returned to South Africa in 2003.

Andile had become an MK commander and later joined the South African National Defence Force; sadly, he passed away in a car accident.

During the early 1990s, following the unbanning of the ANC, the release of political prisoners and the return of exiles, Rita was finally reunited with her children.

Sometimes Ma Rita's memory wanders. One memory she returns to and can't seem to help dwelling on is the second forced removal from the family home, which happened in 1984. Having returned to Mogopa village in Ventersdorp in the North West, her father again experienced the jarring trauma of being forcibly removed from land that had been in their family since 1912. It is a trauma that she remembers easily, decades later. She was as tall as the tyres on the truck that came to raze their homes. The community was surrounded by police officers, front doors were kicked in and the removals began. Women and children were carried to waiting trucks. Tribal leaders were handcuffed and thrown into police vans. In the frenzy, many people sold their livestock to the white farmers waiting to occupy their land for next to nothing, fearing that they would lose any livestock they had reared.

She says

> My father was going to be removed from his house and they bundled him into a car. We were not there, but we left our cattle in the kraal and they took all our furniture. We had so many cows and our furniture (that remained) was all broken. When my father went to get his money (compensation), it was so little.

Held at gunpoint and forced into trucks and buses with a few possessions, they were taken to Pachsdraai in the North West.

Rita counts voting on 27 April 1994 as a vindication of her many years of effort. She was elected to the Gauteng Provincial Council and deployed to the Council of Provinces in Cape Town. In 1999 and 2004, she was elected to the National Assembly, where she served on various committees, including Rural Development and Labour.

Despite a life of hardships, Rita is still able to say:

> This is not my story. It's the story of all the people who did not ac-
> cept apartheid, who were fighting apartheid. They are still there. It's the
> story of all the people who know how it feels to be kicked from the back
> while you are digging the wealth of the country. It's the story of all those
> women, the mothers, who worked in the suburbs, in the kitchens, kneel-
> ing down, scrubbing the floors, doing washing, ironing for nothing. For
> no salary at all.

Rita retired from Parliament in 2004. In honour of the Ndzangas the ANC
Senoane branch was renamed the Lawrence Ndzanga branch.

She still lives in the house she shared with Lawrence on Koma Road, Senoane, Soweto. "In the country, right now, we never lived like the way we are living now," she tells me. "We have got lives, really. We wanted our dignity back."

She dismisses any consideration of psychological help. "I didn't have any
counselling. I only went to a doctor when I felt pain or if I didn't have tablets. I still take tablets." She gestures to her forearm.

> If you see my arm when I fell (after she was dropped onto the bricks
> and fell on the gas pipe), I could feel the pain from here. Sometimes I
> can hardly pick my hand up. It's painful. Nowadays, I am tired. People
> think we don't want to associate anymore, but it is because of these sick-
> nesses. All that, it comes from detention without trial.

****

In 2020, I pay a visit to Ma Rita with Shanthie and her husband, Dominic.
Ma Rita's granddaughter Laurette, Thami's daughter, has arranged a visit
between the old friends on an afternoon. Rita's youngest son, Cecil, has also
come for a visit from Mpumalanga.

In a year, Ma Rita has grown smaller and she is less lucid and more frail
than I have seen her, but she is thrilled to see her old comrade. They speak
about their work and time and Dominic serves as a thought-starter about
the events from 50 years before.

She shows us photographs of her sons, Andile and Jongi.

Cecil remembers the various detentions of his parents, even though he
was a young boy. There is a quiet pain on his face as he thinks about his
childhood. But there were also brave, happy moments.

> I remember the SB car across the road – a small VW Beetle. It was
> there before we left to school, and when we got back home it was still
> there. I don't know what they were watching for. Sometimes they
> would follow us.

He and his schoolmates would work as runners. "There were lots of side roads around the house, it wasn't as built up as it is now," Cecil says.

> My parents would send us to meet friends or comrades passing through into exile, or collecting pamphlets at the top of the road, and we would bring them all the way around, through the back, and the SB didn't know a thing. They tried a lot of tricks. But we were aware of them and I think in fact we overworked them. We knew what we were doing, he beams.

While his parents were an anomalous political family in the area, people quietly supported the movement even with silence and camaraderie.

> There were some neighbours who would tell their kids "Don't play with those kids," meaning us, but it was tough for the cops to infiltrate and recruit around here. There were one or two impimpis but we always knew who it was. At my father's funeral there were people brought by the cops. A few boys and I were sitting in a car at the graveyard, just us kids. But we were very aware that an informer was sitting with us in the car, so we knew what to say and not say.

When they were still teenagers, the Ndzanga children went into exile in Swaziland, Mozambique and Tanzania.

> We went to school in Mazimbu and were trained by the MK. Later we also moved to join the ANC in exile and worked for the ANC until our return back to South Africa in 1995. My mother was in parliament as an MP with President Nelson Mandela and later during Mr Mbeki's presidency. My sister Thami came back with her daughter Laurette.

The third generation of Ndzangas, Laurette was born and grew up in Germany. The young accountant has prepared a spread for the ladies to reminisce over today – fresh fruit and canapés, and a range of pastries. Her grandmother does not have much of an appetite, but the food revives a memory that makes Laurette so uncomfortable that she has to leave the room.
Ma Rita says:

> There was a time when we lived in Sophiatown. I went to school but in the holidays we went to work for those whites who were staying nearby. I used to take a bus, and then we work, clean a stoep for two bob or two and six shillings. It was hard to be a black person those days. Something I did hate about that: I saw this blue dish near the water tap. They told me to eat my lunch in there. And I thought, something is making me not eat in this dish. The next day when I came to work, I saw the dog eating from the same dish. How can people do that to other people? To them there was no difference between a dog and a black person …

She trails off, retreating into her memories, and after a few minutes, shaking her head, she says, "Some of the scars are so deeply rooted."

This is one of the reasons why her speech at Winnie Mandela's funeral in 2018 was a strained, impassioned one. "They who speak ill of those who are late, they are mad," she tells us.

> I worked with Winnie for many years. She was in trouble, just like any other woman, like any other young girl. With her husband away, she had her children and she was struggling just like me. I don't know why people can say such things about people who are late. Winnie was not a bad person. To remember where we come from and where we are now, that is important.

Rita Ndzanga said in 2019: 'This is not my story. It's the story of all the people who did not accept apartheid, who were fighting apartheid. They are still there … It's the story of all those women, the mothers, who worked in the suburbs, in the kitchens, kneeling down, scrubbing the floors, doing washing, ironing for nothing. For no salary at all.' Picture: Alaister Russell/*Sunday Times*

Notes

1 Ahmed Kathrada Foundation.
2 [IDAF archive].

7 Nondwe Mankahla

We don't want men who wear skirts under their trousers. If they don't want to act, let us women exchange garments with them.[1]

Lillian Ngoyi

There is a familiarity about New Brighton township on the outskirts of Port Elizabeth (PE). It is scorching in the summer, the maze of sandy streets and unplanned clusters of houses busy on a weekday. I work out that we are not far away from legendary actor and activist John Kani's home. The township has often been mentioned in the theatre and dramas that depicted the early days of the struggle. The Eastern Cape, as it is known now, was the heartbeat of the resistance movement, after all. A few months have passed since Winnie Mandela's funeral and I am here to visit the last of the remaining four women.

Nondwe "Brysina" Mankahla, was born nearby, in the Red Location, on 28 August 1935. Today her home is off an unpaved path, dusty with the white sand typical of the area. Outside her gate, a neighbour sells a man a glass of beer, despite the sun making an appearance barely a few hours prior. Her house is well appointed and impeccably tidy. Greeted by her daughter, Phila, who is in her 50s, I am told that the family is mourning the death of Nondwe's eldest daughter, Nombuso. I offer condolences.

A spritely, chubby Nondwe, 84, can't believe it has been 50 years since her detention when I remind her. It was one of two imprisonments that marked her life as an activist, and as a mother, she says.

We drive to the PE beachfront, the famous wind whistling casually in the early morning. Nondwe points out a grocery store where she once worked in the town, and the infamous Sanlam building where she and many others were interrogated, including Steve Biko before he was murdered.

She says her life was ordinary, but her mother, Nellie, was involved in political protest as long as she could remember.

> We lived in Middledrift, in the Mnqaba location. Then in 1945, when I was in Sub A, my mother wanted to come back again to Port Elizabeth to live with my father and this is how we ended up in New Brighton.

DOI: 10.4324/9781003228905-8

Nondwe is one of eight children whom her mother had to care for after her father died in 1952. 'In the 1950s it was fashionable, in a way, that young people became active in the ANC. Even when I was in school I was anxious to know about it, what was this ANC? I worked as a cleaner at the technical college, because I couldn't get an education ... I fell pregnant at a young age. When my father died, I was young, a teenager, but I had to work. My mother was a hard worker. She would make vetkoek and smileys (braaied sheep's heads) and sell it to the factory workers.

> I first heard of the African National Congress in 1952. I was about seventeen. We heard the volunteers singing in the streets that we should join them, and Tata (Wilton) Mkwayi and others preaching in the streets that we should go to a meeting. I wasn't involved until the Defiance Campaign. We all wanted to be in the Defiance Campaign, although we didn't know what the source was and what we were defying.

She laughs and continues:

> We just went there as children. That was June 26, 1952. There would be sleepovers, we would spend the whole night praying, then in the morning you go home. I continued being just a volunteer until I realised in discussions and meetings what the ANC was all about. We would go together in groups, singing *Senzeni na.*

> Senzeni na?
> Sono sethu, ubumnyama?
> Sono sethu yinyaniso?
> Sibulawayo
> Mayibuye iAfrica
> *
> What have we done?
> Our sin is that we are black?
> Our sin is the truth
> They are killing us
> Let Africa return

> Those songs were being sung by people who would go to break the law (in protest), *Senzeni na, Mayibuye iAfrica.* We would listen to speeches given by Mama Florence Matomela and other leaders, giving speeches trying to tell that generation what the ANC was about.

Nondwe decided to join the ANC as a volunteer, but there is one incident that stands out in her mind which bolstered her commitment to the movement.

> It was October 1952. I was selling vetkoeks (doughnuts), maas (sour milk) and rosterkoek (bread) at the hostel. There was a 2.30 pm train

that came through New Brighton and there was a big noise. There was a man arrested for having a tin of paint. In those days a black man was not supposed to be seen with something that a black man couldn't have or own. You had to produce papers. The arguments started there with the guards and station policemen asking him where he got the paint. He told them that he bought it, but they didn't believe him.

Everyone was watching this man fighting with the police. People took stones from the tracks and threw them at the police. We followed them to the station's security office. A man by the name of Du Preez, who was in charge there, didn't say anything. He just got out his gun and fired. People fell. This carried on just outside the train station. The fight moved to the hostel. Guns firing and people falling.

This was a year in PE when there was rioting, when shops and cinemas were burned down in protest.

"I joined the Youth League and worked as a volunteer. We would go in groups, door-to-door, telling people about the ANC, what it did and what it stood for." Nondwe has a straight-forward way of talking. "We were telling people," she says. "Sometimes they didn't even care what we were talking about. But at least they listened."

In 1955, she was part of the contingent who assisted the Congress of the People with the gathering of viewpoints and listening to the hopes for the movement and reparations for the country, to be adopted into the Freedom Charter. "So many people in rural areas, and in town, didn't know about the struggle. We would say that the ANC could govern in the next years. It was like we were telling them a myth." The communities asked for livestock and homes, land for farming.

Others would say they want to be free and be like whites, to walk on the pavements, because in those days you wouldn't see a black person walking on the pavements with white people. Other elders would say that they want to be free because "this land is the land of our forefathers. We hear that our land was sold to Jan van Riebeeck. He showed them mirrors and would take a cow for showing them themselves in the mirror." That's what they told me.

The enforcement of Bantu Education, the carrying of the passbook, or *dompas*, and the forced removals under the Group Areas Act were top of mind for Nondwe and the growing group of comrades in the area. "In Korsten black people were living with a mixture of whites, Muslims, coloureds and Indians. But they started this division and rules of segregation. Everyone who was a non-white was sent to plank townhouses," she says.

Nondwe worked closely with ANC leader Govan Mbeki, particularly as her work involved the sale and distribution of banned newspapers.

Oom Gov would take a picture and take incidents (stories) around it from people, then send it to Cape Town where Real Printing and Publishing was, and then to Johannesburg. I was a volunteer selling the paper. As volunteers we had to wear our black and khaki uniform with a rosette. Men wore a khaki suit with a rosette. We were disciplined. We were told not to drink or smoke. We were told to do everything with respect. Even as young people, boyfriends and girlfriends weren't something that should be important to you. The struggle had to come first.

Even when it was dangerous to continue the work, the volunteers marched and often faced police armed with live ammunition.

Nondwe's memories of that time are very clear and she is articulate in describing them.

In 1955 we had celebrations around the signing of the Freedom Charter. We protested against Bantu Education and the *dompas* (those things were so big, the size of a handbag!). We were always collecting, working together to raise funds for the movement. I used to distribute pamphlets and notices for meetings, and after work we would have our meetings.

Aspects of her activism started out as a form of employment. "There was a paper called the *New Age*. The movement needed this paper to get out, everywhere." She gestures widely with short, stocky arms.

After work on a Wednesday and Friday I would go to New Brighton station to sell the *New Age*. But then I would also collect the money for our activities and families who needed help. On weekends, we would have rallies.

She found full-time employment at the printing and publishing company that was producing the *New Age*, *Fighting Talk* and the *Pondo Revolt*. This was of course another illegal act under the apartheid laws, as she was aiding in the distribution of banned material, but she speaks casually about it and the brave act of distributing these publications, which informed comrades about the progress of the struggle which, by the 1960s, had gone underground, and to garner support and provide inspiration. "We would get bundles from Johannesburg and I was distributing during the rallies," she says.

The paper was brought to Port Elizabeth by passenger train on Thursdays. I would collect the paper from the station and then distribute them in zonal areas. I had other volunteers – people who did not work – who sold the paper. I would put the papers in that office where Oom Gov worked and then distribute them.

Nondwe says she often went undetected because of her petite build. "Before the ANC was banned, people would get detained and released. I would be left behind because of my small physique. They would think I am a child," she smiles.

Subscribers to the newspaper were multiracial, across the city.

> But they could not collect the paper because they did not want to be seen. What would happen is that I would be given the *New Age* paper and a list of people I should deliver them to quietly. Every week I would take the paper to town to people who were distributing it.

The newspaper was also used as messenger service between banned people.

> There was a Chinese grocer who sold the paper for us, and an Indian man who had a barbershop who distributed from there. They were also ANC members. From the barbershop I would come back with a fruit parcel to give to Oom Gov. It would be an apple or banana. But in this fruit, there was something hidden. I didn't have a problem because I was just carrying a fruit basket and my papers so the police were not paying any attention to me.

As the newspapers were banned, others were created. Nondwe remained a messenger for ten years. "We carried on, focusing on the townships, playing hide-and-seek," she says.

> In 1962 Oom Gov and others disappeared. I was alone in the (ANC) office with Caleb Mayekiso and a few people from the Textile and Food and Canning Workers unions. There was a policeman who was watching us. He saw me on the bus one day and he said: "You are always hiding. Today, I am arresting you".

She wasn't given a chance to go home, to collect clothing or to tell her mother and children that she was being detained.

> I got a chance to shout to some people when we were passing the Baakens Bridge. People were alarmed but I said: "I am Nondwe Mankahla! Please go tell them at home in Ferguson, I have been arrested. They don't know where I am. I am at Walmer".

Surprisingly, someone heard and alerted her mother. "Even in court I would shout by force and tell them who I am and ask them to tell them at home, so my mother knew where I was."

Nondwe was detained for the first time in 1963 for a year, as an awaiting-trial prisoner.

We were a big group in three vans. We would sing on the road giving people an idea where we were being taken. And people would follow us. I was in a group of 74 that was sent to Graaff-Reinet, with other women. We were not sentenced.

When her trial date came, she was surprised to see her mother Nellie on trial too. While she was locked up Nondwe's four young children had supposedly been in the care of their grandmother. "I got a fright. I asked who was with the kids, and Mama said, 'God will be there.'"

The time in prison stretched on, but at least she was not alone. There were a few other political prisoners in her cell. In a light moment, she remembers the political prisoners creating a "rugby match" by passing ants' crumbs of mieliepap to play with.

In Kroonstad she got her first taste of political detention. 'In Kroonstad we stayed in single cells. When they let us out it would be to take our tubs and wash them and get air for a few minutes. Then we would bathe and food would come. It was pap, always pap. There were times when we would get vegetables, carrots and cabbage and other things. But we didn't know the vegetables were old. The following day we would get sick and have upset tummies.

We were not working. It is boring. There is no Bible. The single cell is small. You had to clean yourself while the other person is standing there. It was open, so the officers could see us at any time. And it was so cold in the Free State. They would let us out when it was freezing ... we were told to go out and do exercises. There was this old lady, Mrs Matomela (an activist and leader), who was a diabetic. She needed to be injected with insulin. They would take their time to come inject her. If she is not injected, she would react to the food and get ill. We felt so bad. Then there was Mrs Mabuda, who had arthritis ...

The floors were cement and icy cold on the body. "We even tried hunger strikes. Then in 1965 we finally got work, to sew the covers for the army's water bottles." She pauses, remembering, then adds with morbid satisfaction: "Every time we would finish a can we would say, 'Curse it.' Mama Marwey would say: 'The person carrying this bottle must go and die on the border.'

The detentions didn't do much to quell the fight in her. She and her mother were released, and their political work continued.

Then on 31 May 1969 the security branch knocked on the door of the supermarket where she worked as an assistant.

First they came and told me: "We would like you to work with us. We have some guys who mentioned your name." I asked, "What? How can I work with *you*?" They said I must testify against those comrades. *Haai*, I couldn't say no or yes.

She claps her hands together.

> Shan (Pillay), who was my boss, he said, "Brysina, you must be careful."
> He knew I was in jail previously and he had given me a job, even though
> the special branch was after me. He told me not to answer them and they
> must come back after a few days so I can think about it.

They arrived in their heavy boots and khakis a few days later. "When I
refused, they said, 'We are taking you for further questioning.' I thought to
myself, This is goodbye."

Over the years, many comrades had been killed in detention and Nondwe
feared this was her last call.

> I went home to collect a few things, to change. My dresses, some under-
> wear. I don't remember having a coat, a jersey maybe. They took me to
> police cells in Walmer. They won't let you spend more (than a few) days
> in the same place. They take you from place to place so people don't
> notice you and your family can't find you. At midnight they took me to
> Sanlam building and asked me, and asked me, and asked me questions.

She pauses, appearing fatigued from reliving the time. 'They asked me if I
know someone, and someone else, all these people in Joburg. They showed
me photos, and then they asked me about meeting Joyce Sikhakhane. You
can't say that you don't know. They don't like that ... they start to shake you
up. There was a box, like a trunk. You climb on it, then onto some bricks
and you stand on those bricks until you tell them what they want to know.
They know everything, but they want to get it from you to use as evidence. I
refused. They didn't get anything from me,' she says proudly.

> They continued until I thought I was going to die. They would give you
> breathing space until they get new information and then take you again
> in those rooms in Sanlam. My friend, MaMbele, was badly hurt, with
> blood coming out of her mouth. My feet were so swollen ...

Nondwe had met Joyce but the meeting was so brief and innocuous she
hadn't realised it was anything of concern.

> When I met Joyce Sikhakhane, she said, "Winnie asked me to come to
> you because the movement was far away from the Eastern Cape." This
> woman came as a social worker, to ask if we were getting any food par-
> cels. Another time, someone else came and said they had been sent by
> Nelson's wife. And I asked: "Who is that?" They said: "Winnie." I said:
> "I haven't worked with Nelson's wife."

While Nondwe cannot recall who it was that visited her, the woman had said
that Winnie had sent her to help find activists to go into exile. Nondwe was

also offered the chance to leave PE. "I said I cannot because I don't know anyone overseas. And I just came back from jail (her first detention). I had stayed away from home for far too long."

> "I remember the lady said, 'Now, Nondwe, we are on this (mission) trying to look for you guys to help because you can't get work if you are in politics.' Because in the 1960s people were scared, there was no work. I didn't get a job, until 1966. So we just spoke," she says. "But those two meetings, that's how they caught us. It was a few minutes, but that's how they got me. They had photos."

"After two days they took me to Humansdorp." This quaint town in the Eastern Cape was where Nondwe feared she would meet her end. "If you are in those cells, nobody can see you. Nobody knows you are there." Her mother and two children had no idea where she was.

> You don't see another person. The commandant gives you food. Then you get a bucket of water and a toilet bucket. Sometimes they leave you for the whole day, or two days. You can't sleep. Sometimes they would come at midnight to wake you up, to make you talk. I had nothing to say.

She adds adamantly: "Really – I had nothing to say."

The security branch officers would slap and beat her with open hands, to not mark her with evidence of their violence, she says.

> They showed me more photos. That's where they caught me. I was in a photo with some people who were banned … Samson Ndou (the first accused in the trial). I met him once before we got arrested. They said, "Now we got you!"

Nondwe was forced to agree to testify in court.

> They said I must testify that Ndou was trained as a guerrilla, that he was dangerous. I just agreed, to avoid more beatings. They went to my mum's house and said she must pack enough things for me because I am going away for a long, long time. I was in the cells, they went without me, and I didn't see her or my kids. I only saw the suitcase later, so at least they knew.

She met battered and bruised South Africa Communist Party members in the vans they would share on the 1,000 km journey to the Transvaal, as Gauteng was known then.

> They bought milk and bread for us and asked us if we are ready to give evidence. I said to them that I am not giving evidence against my people. I said I am not doing it. (In the vehicle) no one wanted to say

anything to anyone. Everyone had their own decision to make. And I said to myself again, I am not giving evidence when I get there.

The journey was almost a day long.

> They took us to Pretoria. I didn't know the city at all. At the cells they separated us. You don't know who is next door. It could be a criminal, but we were next to each other, in solitary confinement.

I ask if she was afraid, leaving her children and her mother. She shrugs dismissively. "*Bashile amabantwana.* I left my two children. We didn't think of being scared. We didn't know anything, we just went to the prison," she says. Later, however, she would share the emotion around this with me.

****

The cells were grey, cement floor, and not much else. The draught that came in under the door brought the cold. There was mesh over a single small window, and a naked light bulb, very bright – for others, no light. Hours became days, became weeks and months with little changing for Nondwe apart from her mind running riot.

> What did I do for a year? *Sjoe.* In the morning, I would do my exercises and my loo, then after wash myself in the bucket. I had to get soap, when I could. I had a toothbrush and toothpaste sometimes, but that would get finished and you don't know when you would get it again. Then, I would wash my clothes and fold them neatly. If you put the clothes under the blanket and sit on it, it would take out some of the wrinkles. Before the loo bucket comes out, the breakfast has already been there waiting.

Nondwe has a forthright way of storytelling. She says

> Some days, they take away the bucket early, other days it is with you when you eat. You don't see anything or anyone. I don't even know who took the bucket. The room was so small. We were supposed to have time to exercise but we didn't get that. Not a single day did I see anyone else. Their plan is that nobody must know who you are. Whenever a door is open you must stand up to attention as a prisoner. Even if you don't see anyone, you have to do it,

She believes that lying on the cold floor made her feel ill for most of the day. "If you were a favourite you got an extra mat. Otherwise, we had three thin blankets."

She, too, feared anything that was given to them. "If they gave you medication, you didn't take it. We didn't trust them. Something in the food was not right. Maybe it was the cold, maybe the food, but I know for a whole year, my menstruation stopped."

The international community frowned on South Africa's detention and treatment of political prisoners, and expected them to be treated well if they were detained.

> Every second week a magistrate would come around to the cells and ask, "What is your complaint?" He would try to speak English, Xhosa and Zulu. After four times of telling him my complaints with no results, I said, "I'm not answering anything" and I just looked at him. Eventually I said, "I've been telling you, I don't get exercise, I don't get anything from my people, no visits. My people are far away, not even a letter arrives. Why must I say I'm all right?"

That resistance was futile, Nondwe would learn.

> During the day I walked, up and down the cell. It's small (1.5 by 4 m). One time I found two pins. I took a piece of thread and tried to crochet. Then, I would undo it, and do it again. We had more than a year of this, only interrogation in between and once or twice to the Synagogue for the trial.

In 2018, sitting down to a meal of chicken and vegetables with the smell and sounds of the ocean nearby, she speaks about the unpalatable conditions of health and nutrition in prison.

"Food …," she shakes her head.

> Pap in the morning, hard mealies for lunch, pap and veg (in the) evening. If there was meat, you just saw a hole (in the starch), the meat was gone before it got to you. Whether it was Christmas or not, we didn't know. Once when I was in detention in Port Elizabeth, we got a raisin bun for Christmas. But that was our food in Pretoria, every day. If I don't want to eat, I still had to eat. If there is a worm in the vegetables, or sand, I still had to eat. First you see a worm and get *naar* (nauseous), then you just move it to the side … or you could eat it, she laughs.

All four of the women have told me the solitude and loneliness were far worse than the beatings, putrid food and unliveable conditions.

The only time the detainees could communicate was in the early hours of the morning, or late at night. Despite thick doors and cement separating them, they could hear each other. Some shared recipes. "There's a carrot cake recipe I still use today, I think it was from (the trade unionist) Mrs (Frances) Baard … carrots, raisins, flour and jam," Nondwe quips.

After a time, there were clues about other political prisoners interspersed in the prison community.

There was a time in the evening when we could talk in the cells. When the warders are gone, you tell your stories by singing in your own language – "My name is Nondwe from Port Elizabeth" – and they wouldn't know. We would sometimes know who was around by passing the Bible around. We would share the Bible. That helped me, because those people looking after us in the jail wouldn't tell us who was there and who wasn't there. So we asked them to pass the Bible to someone and if they do, then you get it back, you know that person is still here. But the warders worked it out. Once they noticed, that stopped.

But in that time, we found slowly that there are so many of us in for politics. We spoke to one another. "Where are you from?" I would answer that I'm from Port Elizabeth. If they said, "I'm here in jail overnight," you know it is not a political prisoner. There was a small gap in the door, I used to peep and peep but you couldn't see much. The door was so thick.

She once got a clue of a visitor nearby. "I heard someone going in and out the whole night," she whispers, as if she is back in those quiet cells.

The women prisoners said she was coming from hospital. Then she was transferred next door to me and I heard them say, "Winnie, are you okay?" so I knew it was Winnie Mandela. I didn't know what she looked like. I never even saw her face but I had read about Winnie before. We never met, before. Once I found out it was Winnie, I took my mat and my blankets and leaned myself against the wall.

Nondwe continues:

We didn't even know each other's faces. When we talked, I imagined what Winnie was like and she wondered how I looked. We would speak all night, sitting against those walls. We spoke about the children, often. It was heartsore, so we tried to stop talking about kids. We spoke about who was around, who was arrested, or in exile. I told her about my work with Oom Gov in PE, that I was the secretary. Winnie told her stories. She went to hospital often, she was not well.

And she asked if I knew that Mr Mayekiso had died. I was alarmed then. And I asked what happened. She told me he was arrested and on the next day he was found hanged in the cell. It was the first time I heard of such a thing. We carried on and talked through the crack. It's not even a crack. I would put the enamel chamber pot and a blanket on the corner and lean and talk to her.

The mental warfare was not lost on Nondwe.

There were some people next door. Three sets of women sentenced to death. I was next to them. One had killed her husband and the other two had killed their employers. I heard their cries as they went to the gallows. Every time there was a priest to let them pray, but he would say: "You are going to die. You did this." How do you think it feels to be there, next door, knowing we might be next to go to the gallows? she asks.

She remembers activist Frances Baard. "She had a nervous breakdown in Nylstroom. She said someone is speaking to her in her ear." She indicates graphically and gives a deep sigh.

"Our trial was very long, *sjoe*, nearly two years. You wouldn't wear prisoners' clothes. In detention you wear your own clothes. Sometimes you get the chance of doing your washing, inside the cell, not even outside," she says.

The lack of hygiene and chills made her feel ill. "I felt sick for a long time. Underneath the door, there is a cold wind. The cells are not cold only because of cement. Those draughts under ..." and she gestures with a hand, although it doesn't need further explaining.

One day in December, the cell door opened.

When I was taken to testify I had an old dress of mine on. I had no panty or bra and I didn't even wash. I was doing my exercises in the cell and then the door opened. I had nothing on the head, like a mad person. Luckily I had plaited my hair. They said, "*Kom!*" and when I asked where, they said, "Don't ask". I didn't finish my porridge, I thought I'll come back and eat it, cold or what, I don't care I'm so used to it.

She remembers a vehicle in front of the prison.

Everyone was shaken to see me like that, as if I was just taken out of a hole. When I went there (to the Old Synagogue) I saw all the accused, the 22. One guy from Eastern Cape (Ndou) I knew, but I last saw him five years before.

Ndou had been training at MK (uMkhonto we Sizwe ("Spear of the Nation") camps out of South Africa.

I said, "It's my comrade" and they shouted, "You still call this man comrade? He is a terrorist!" They thought I would testify and tell the judge. They thought I was going to fear them. I knew that I'm not going to give any evidence.

The memory of her deception makes Nondwe chuckle. She made her pleas to the judge without holding back.

I said, "All I know is that if you have agreed to give evidence for the state, number one, you don't sit in jail. You go home and come back on the day of the trial. Number two, you don't eat the nonsense I ate there."

He (Justice Bekker) asked me to tell him what I ate. I said: "I ate pap and mealies. I only ate better food once, when I arrived, with spinach, pap and meat. When I told them I was not giving evidence I was sent back to my old diet." The inspectors were red in the faces.

Nondwe further embarrassed prison officials by telling the judge how she was coerced to use a state lawyer who did not have her best interests at heart.

We were not allowed to stand in front of a judge without a lawyer, but the lawyer they (the state) would give you meant you would just go to jail. This guy came to me, to ask if I am PE and said, "I understand you didn't want to give evidence. Would you like me to represent you?" I said, "After arresting me last year, *now* you are giving me a lawyer? No."

He said, "You cannot go to the judge without an advocate." I said, "Well, you will wait for my letter from my lawyer. If you represent me, I don't think I will be free. Why didn't you free me when I was in detention?"

In the Old Synagogue Nondwe asked Justice Bekker for permission to

write home to Port Elizabeth to instruct (George) Bizos so I can be amongst the other people (in the trial). When I asked the other prison officials, they swore at me. So, I asked the judge for permission to write to my lawyer. The judge said: "Yes, you have permission." Then Justice Bekker asked again, "Are you giving evidence?" I just said, "No."

The judge adjourned the court for a recess. "When he came back and said, 'Do you know if you don't testify you will get jailed for many years?' I just shut up," says Nondwe.

Shortly after Shanthie's and Nondwe's lack of testimony, the trial was dismissed.

Nondwe says she tried to maximise the time out of the cell.

I wanted to go to the loo and someone escorted me to this shed. Then I saw outside, there were lots of people from PE. I wanted to see if my mum was there, but the warders said "Don't look." They were all scared of the way I looked, anyway, after all that time in the dark cell. But they also told me, "You have broken the law, you are in contempt of court," because I didn't testify, she says.

"We had to sleep over without any clothes in the Pretoria holding cells. We were just given a blanket. After the trial they sent me back in for another 90 days."

****

When she was finally released Nondwe went back to PE by train, travelling in the third-class carriage.

> I was thinking that I might die in jail. I thought I'll never see my children. In the first prison (her earlier detention), I really thought of them. But when you volunteer yourself ... (in Pretoria) I had to try my best to forget about them. When I was released, in June 1960, they told me to "Stop your nonsense of going in and out" (of jail).

She was so afraid of being rearrested that she got off at a station before her final stop and walked the rest of the way home.

> I found my sister-in-law who is a nurse, she took care of me. I sat down, then I started to shake. I couldn't sleep, and I was just shaking all the time. For two or three months, I was talking and shivering, shaking. I couldn't hold anything. I had to see the doctor. They felt it was a lack of nutrition. I had to take multivitamins and eat healthy food like cheese and lettuce on brown bread, which was expensive, but I think my body was not nourished. When I was released, I was not well, especially in my mind.

She tears up remembering seeing her children after 18 months. "My children, they didn't know me. I left them when they were very young ... when I remember, that's when I get hurt. I don't like to talk about it." She stops to wipe her tears for those young children who couldn't recognise their mother. "In the detention, I really thought of them. But when you volunteer yourself ... I had to forget about them. It was sad when I came back. Now, they know me." She exhales.

Nondwe doesn't regret her time to the cause, but she says she knows the impact it had on her children. She was not attached to their fathers, and her children were cared for by her mother and her sister, who had kids of her own. She believes her own scars are not as significant as their emotional ones. She says it may have contributed to the demise of her elder daughter's mental health. "My children, they questioned why we were not okay after I came back. I couldn't do much to educate them." Yet, there were two teachers among them, and her daughter Phila worked for the provincial government.

From 1970, Nondwe says, she got back into life and she spent the rest of her working life caring for her children. For many years she was still on the radar of the apartheid state, however. "Those people, the special branch, they still followed me. They will trail your car wherever you are, even until 1983 I would see them. I used to hate those people, following me even to work," she says.

It was difficult to find work after being released. "People were scared, if you went to jail for politics. I didn't get a job straight away, but the Black

Sash helped us." She eventually managed to get a job in a grocery store, and then a hardware store. She worked in the hardware store for 30 years – and after 1994 she became a veteran.

Nondwe never married. "It's not my tradition to marry someone even if we had a child together," she laughs. She was once in a relationship with a married man, a salesman who had a family in the Transkei.

> He wanted me to stay with him but people told his wife to watch, he was seeing this woman who was in jail. When we come home from jail, men are also scared of you. Ag, anyway, I was not interested in husbands.

She grows quiet for a few moments, reflecting. "Only now, when I reached my 60s, life is normal," she says. "We don't meet our comrades often. In 1994, I saw Joyce; and Madiba and Winnie visited. We had to laugh together after a long time." The next visit, they cried together. "I could not, not be there, I was so sad," she says.

Fifty years on, I ask Nondwe how she feels about her contribution.

"My kids also want to know why I'm not up there with the others (politicians). I don't care," she said dismissively. "When we were young, we were not equal in this country. I saw myself growing up like that, and it was not the way it should be," she says.

Nondwe Mankahla in July 1992. Picture: *Evening Post/The Herald*.

Apart from what is happening now, I'm okay. Young people, hey, they don't know about the really bad times. Sometimes when I see things going badly, I think What did I do this for? There was a chance I wouldn't have been alive. It is sad because ANC now is collapsing. All these guys of the 1980s and 1990s, they don't care about real politics. They have never been arrested, or been in jail and in solitary. There is no discipline. They want houses – and not even with small land. I had to work for where I live now. I didn't even get a RDP house because I was unmarried. But I'm not angry about that.

I didn't do it to be famous. I never think of that, and I never expected it. You know, I think my strength comes from knowing that everything is over. Really, now we are free. It is not about money. I sacrificed all of that for my kids. I'm that type of person. I don't think it is anything special that I did ... I'm not here for compensation. If I do get ... if I don't get ... it's up to their own minds. What comes up is what comes up. I didn't go there for my own rewards. I went for the country.

'We didn't even know each other's faces,' Nondwe Mankahla recalled in 2019 of her time in solitary and discovering that Winnie Madikizela-Mandela was in a nearby cell. 'When we talked, I imagined what Winnie was like and she wondered how I looked. We would speak all night, sitting against those walls. We spoke about the children, often. It was heartsore, so we tried to stop talking about kids.' Picture: Fredlin Adriaan/*The Herald*

Note

1 Ngoyi, 1956.

8 "Rooi Rus" Swanepoel

A malevolent figure hovers over the stories of many political activists in South Africa. His name shows up in historical evidence around the mass campaigns, detention and interrogation – torture – of political detainees. For the women of the Trial of 22, the name of the bulbous-nosed, red-faced architect of the special branch operations elicits a physical reaction decades later.

Swanepoel.

Theunis J "Rooi Rus" Swanepoel died in Roodepoort on the West Rand in 1998, aged 70.

His moniker, "Red Russian," was due to his flushed appearance. The vivid memory of his interrogations lives on in the minds of his victims. Shanthie often has nightmares that feature him, and Joyce uses breathing techniques to calm herself if a memory returns. Nondwe remembers that he travelled to Port Elizabeth to question her. And while Ma Rita dismisses him with a wave of her hand, her experience of him was perhaps the cruellest.

It was Swanepoel who had led the team of security police which raided Liliesleaf farm in Rivonia and arrested the MK (uMkhonto we Sizwe ("Spear of the Nation")) leadership, among them Ahmed Kathrada, Raymond Mhlaba and others.

Evidence at the Truth and Reconciliation Commission (TRC) revealed that after 1960, a special squad of police officers received intensive training in "non-physical" interrogation and counter-interrogation techniques. This coincided with the torture methods and statements elicited from witnesses in the Rivonia Trial. The many strategies developed by the apartheid state to contain resistance to the apartheid system included detention, solitary confinement, torture (both mental and physical) and harassment. Researcher Padraig O'Malley found there was a marked shift to the approach which saw teams working in relay, using sleep deprivation and extended standing on one spot, or the "hard/soft cop" routine, to get information out of the detainee.

A common thread in the stories of detention was the torture techniques of the apartheid government to extract information from detainees and to send

DOI: 10.4324/9781003228905-9

a message of what the result of activism would be. With the government's introduction of the 90-day and 180-day detention laws, detainees frequently reported being mercilessly tortured, particularly if they were suspected of acts of sabotage. This was despite a blanket denial by the state that any form of torture was taking place. Notorious for interrogations that involved meting out torture was a special police unit called the "Sabotage Squad,"[1] O'Malley found.

Swanepoel was known to favour torture involving electrical currents. He was also among those who contributed to Babla Saloojee's "fall" from a window during interrogation in 1964. The apartheid state credited him for "breaking" what it considered a communist threat to South Africa, which could have added to the meaning of his nickname. Former presidential spokesman Mac Maharaj wrote about how Swanepoel tortured him for months in a brutal manner such as it defines the vile nature of the man. A favourite torture method was to make his foe stand naked at the edge of a table in a room known as Die Waarheid Kamer (The Truth Room), hands handcuffed behind him, with his genitals on the table. Swanepoel would hit the genitals hard, and repeatedly, with a blunt object, until the detainee fainted. Mac Maharaj did not crack, incredibly, and he joined the ANC (African National Congress) leadership on Robben Island.

Significantly, there is evidence in the research O'Malley conducted post-apartheid for the TRC that

> a number of officers received further training in interrogation and counter-interrogation techniques in France in about 1968. Officers known to have attended this course include: TJ "Rooi Rus" Swanepoel, Major JJ "Blackie" de Swardt, Hans Gloy, Roelf van Rensberg and Dries Verwey. Apparently, Swanepoel gained his notoriety after torturing some of his captives severely and elicited confessions that culminated in the Rivonia Trial.

The women were detained in 1969, the year after these security officers received the additional training, which puts into perspective their treatment by the security police and by Swanepoel in particular. The evidence reveals a strategy developed and used by the state to use especially harsh methods on political activists.

Shanthie Naidoo's brother Indres was arrested in 1963. "Swanepoel was just a sergeant at that stage," she recalled. "By the time I was detained, he was a major and he was trained abroad by the French. The French were really brutal to the Algerians ..." His newly honed skills included sleep torture. Shanthie said:

> I don't recall how many times I saw him. He was one of the interrogators, but he was the worst. There was one time, they drove me somewhere by car. They wouldn't even tell me where. Later on I worked out that they took me to Pretoria to the Compol building.

The notorious building in Pretorius Street was the home of the special branch. While much of the unit was moved to nearby Wachthuis in 1967, one floor was dedicated to the branch, and many detainees of the time recall torture sessions there – interrogation, as it was called.

"He was the person who interrogated me," Shanthie said.

> I get nightmares about that man, even now. I dream and eventually try to go back to sleep but not often can you go back to sleep after remembering those days. You don't know if it's real it's so vivid.

She paused. Then, her voice sweet but with a bitter edge to it, she said: "They made me stand on bricks for five days without sleep. On the fifth day, he got someone … one of the officers, to push a chair towards me. I think I collapsed." She stopped, then went on: "By this time, I had lost touch with reality. I was hallucinating about flying in a plane. I'd never left the country. I'd never flown. But they took it as evidence of some terrorist activity." She gave me a wry smile.

> I must've been talking aloud. They gave me something to drink and I slept in a camp bed that Friday night. When I got up it was like the floor wasn't there. I don't know what it was that they gave me.

We sat in silence for a short while, a breeze rustling the bougainvillea tree nearby.

"When you are in the situation you cry. You think of everything. You pray," she said, with a furrowed brow.

O'Malley wrote:

> Swanepoel was one of the most prominent members of staff in this infamous unit and his career, endorsed by the state, typifies the actions of the squad. It conducted interrogations throughout the country, employing methods such as applying electric shocks, brutal assault, burning, breaking bones, hanging the suspect upside-down from an open window in a multi-storey block and making him stand in the same position without sleep or food for long periods of up to 60 hours.

"Deaths in detention (20 men between 1960 and 1969 alone, and many more thereafter) were usually labelled as 'suicide' or 'died of natural causes'. At the inquests that followed the government was absolved of all blame."[2]

It is in light of this, and the fact that the women of the 1969 trial were never charged because they refused to give evidence against each other, that their courage needs to be understood. They were exposed to lengthy and frequent sessions of torture in detention, which was renewed unhesitatingly. They were placed under the care of the security police.

Swanepoel chose to play the bad cop. Giving his lieutenants free rein while he was away, he would return with his angry red face, bringing it to

eye level with the detainee while screaming into his or her face. His trainees were either a little more humane or well versed in pretending kindness.
There was always one who was a little softer, who would let them sit for a
few minutes – in Winnie's case, she was allowed to put her head between
her knees to relieve the dizziness. He would show compassion, trying to
coax a response from the detainee. Then Swanepoel would return and
continue the assault. At the next moment of kindness, the detainee might
crack. "Logic is lost, reason is confused. Truth is mixed with lies, and
truth and lies become one,"[3] they reported of the interrogation and solitary confinement.

Nondwe consented to testify – although she didn't follow through – after
being slapped, beaten, kicked, "but never where it (would) leave scars."

The brick torture was a favourite. It entailed two bricks placed together in
a "V" shape, on which the detainee had to somehow try and perch – on their
arches or however possible – to find their balance.

Joyce's face turned sour when she remembered. "I was interrogated by
Rooi Rus Swanepoel, in the Compol building . . . that torture house," she
snorted.

> There were bricks on the floor and a small desk. He pulled out a pistol
> from a drawer. And he pointed it at me and said, "You – stand on the
> bricks." I did, but you can't balance. It was sort of two bricks for each
> foot, so you just wobble. They kept asking, "What is it you are doing?"
> "What was the discussion you had with John in Commissioner Street?"
> I kept repeating that there wasn't anything one was doing.
>
> I was raising funds for families of political prisoners through the
> Anglican church. There wasn't much else. I would collect money and
> distribute it to those families, the money was in envelopes. I don't even
> know how many times I repeated this and how long it was. These things
> are so frightening, that you don't know the time, neh. What tells you of
> the time? You so scared you are going to be shot, she said.

Swanepoel, leading the interrogation, said he would break her if she refused
to talk. "I know how painful it is to break a woman, and I will do it with
you," he threatened her.

She went into some detail at the TRC hearings.

> Today, some of those same apartheid ideologues, the Coetzees, the
> Bothas, the van Wyks, the Swanepoels and others who brutalised the
> majority of South Africans in order to maintain power and control have
> retreated from the State apparatus. Anchored in the sanctuary of their
> lavish homes and farms they watch with cold satisfaction as we, the sur-
> vivors of apartheid, are battling to make South Africa a home for all
> its people, the brutalised, the unemployed, the poor, the unskilled, the
> semi-skilled, the professionals, all and sundry ...

Ma Rita's experience was documented in a paper by the International Defence and Aid Fund for Southern Africa (IDAF) in May 1970.

She was afraid when she saw it was Swanepoel, whose notoriety as one of the harshest interrogators among the security police was shared by other detainees in her cells. She later, under oath, described her torture:

> My first interrogation took place on 16 May. I was taken to a room at the back of Compol Buildings. Major Swanepoel called me by a vulgar name. I kept quiet and did not reply. Other security police continued to question me. Day and night was the same in this room, because of the thick heavy planks covering the windows.
>
> I remained standing. It was late at night. One policeman came round the table towards me, and struck me. I fell to the floor. He said, "*Staan op*," (stand up) and kicked me while I lay on the floor. I lay flat on the floor. They poured water on my face. A new team of interrogators came in – Major Swanepoel and one other. "You will stand on your feet until you decide to speak," they told me. When they began reading other statements to me, I refused to agree to them.
>
> I was taken out for questioning a second time and then for a third time on July 23. In a kitchen, a white security man hit me and I fell, injuring my shoulder. I began to scream …
>
> They closed the windows. I continued screaming. They dragged me to another room, hitting me with their open hands all the time. In the interrogation room, they ordered me to take off my shoes and stand on three bricks. I refused to stand on the bricks. One of the white security police climbed on a chair and pulled me by my hair, and dropped me on the bricks. I fell down and hit a gas pipe. The same man pulled me up by my hair again, jerked me, and I again fell on the metal gas pipe.
>
> They threw water on my face. The man who pulled me by the hair had his hands full of my hair. He washed his hands in the basin. I managed to stand up and then they said, "On the bricks!" I stood on the bricks and they hit me again. While I was on the bricks, I fell. They again poured water on me. I was very tired. I could not stand the assault any longer. I lost all sense of time and I do not know how long these interrogations lasted. I asked to see Major Swanepoel. They said, "*Meid, jy moet praat!*" (Girl, you must talk) I refused.[4]

Rita had no access to lawyers, no visits from her family and no communication from her husband, Lawrence. Throughout her interrogation and confinement, she was told that others had confessed and turned state witness and that she should consider making a statement implicating her fellow activists. Despite her isolation and severe anxiety over the welfare of her family, she resolutely refused to submit a sworn statement which would implicate anyone in a trial.

The squad would tell the detainees they were being sold out by their comrades, that others had accepted payment and gifts and had given in to their demands.

Acclaimed photographer Peter Magubane was told that Winnie was pregnant and would be made to drink poison if he didn't speak up. Otherwise, they would smear her name. On the third round of interrogation, Magubane told the security branch officers that he had great respect for Winnie and that their attempts to have him discredit her were futile.

They would lie about other detainees giving in and turning state witness, or say that the leaders had asked them to give in because they were young and needed to see their families again.

Joyce said later that the psychological profile of the detainees was well known to the squad.

> They studied people. For instance, they would ask you very personal questions during detention and you wondered where did they get this information from. Then you realised later on that they have actually been making a profile of you, in these files, and they would use it to get information from you by filling in gaps.

The torture went on for days, their tormentors taking shifts to watch the women stand. The bricks featured in several interrogation sessions, apart from Winnie Mandela's. It is believed that her prominence in the country and the international eyes on her as a figure of the struggle saved her from some techniques. She was allowed to sit, but not sleep. For five days, the officers would bang on the desks and shout to wake her. Her heart condition might have spared her, but she was mentally anguished – told she was earning money from her activism to buy fashionable clothes, that she was causing her comrades to receive the same interrogation for lesser deeds than hers. While she asked for the charges to be placed solely on her, they did not relent until statements were taken. The officers accused her and taunted her for days, preparing her for their star arrival – Major Swanepoel would walk in when she had cracked, to pry her open entirely.

As soon as she opened her eyes, they began shouting.

> You are nothing but a bitch! You are doing this for money! Do you care for your people who are suffering for you? You were collecting money to buy clothes. Your husband is in prison, who are you tarting yourself up for? Do you think we don't know about you? Nelson must have been desperate to pay lobola for a woman like you.[5]

When it was Swanepoel's turn, he would ask why she was resisting, tell her that it was too late. They had already spread the message to South Africa that she had turned on her people and would be cooperating fully with the police, more so that she would work for them in future. Her political career was over. She would have not a single friend in the ANC, he said, adding sarcastically that she should be grateful that they were keeping her company all night long, because they knew she suffered from insomnia.

Between moments of unconsciousness, Winnie refused, over and over again. Swanepoel thumped on the table and shouted: "For God's sake, give us something! You can't die with all that information! Not before you have told us everything!"[6]

Swanepoel's words were chosen carefully. Mental warfare to make her feel like a miscreant, or an opportunist. The fatigue was meant to coerce her into confusing what was truth and what was not.

> You are going to be broken completely, you are shattered, you are a finished woman. If I had a wife like you, I would do exactly what Nelson has done and go and seek protection in prison. He ran away from you. What kind of women holds meetings up until four o'clock in the morning with other people's husbands? You are the only woman who does this kind of thing.

They presented statements from men who claimed they had had meetings in Nelson's bedroom. "Those days were horrible. I hate to recall them," she would write later.

Swanepoel's voice penetrated her thoughts and she drifted up, as if through water, then forced herself down again, blocking out the voice that fell on her like physical blows. She was fainting more frequently, and knew it was nature's defence against the unendurable. But as soon as she was cognizant again, she was put on her feet and the interrogation continued, for five days and nights, without respite.

Winnie Mandela and Rita Ndzanga were the last of the 22 detainees, rounded up on the same night, for interrogation. Because they were both banned persons and were seen as more prominent activists than the others, the police wanted to extract as much evidence as possible from the others first. Barred from attending meetings or gatherings, both women had made use of go-betweens to keep abreast of what was happening and to convey messages on their behalf. When Winnie failed to respond to the questions put by Swanepoel and his colleagues, they told her Rita had already talked, that they knew everything about meetings at Ndou's storeroom, in Diepkloof, in Alexandra. Meetings in the veld, meetings at her home. They told her not to be a fool, that she would stand alone in the dock, since all the other detainees had already agreed to testify against her.

Lawrence Ndzanga was similarly interrogated, and accounts of his detention mentioned that he was not allowed to use the bathroom for days. He was not to survive his subsequent detention and torture a few years later.

For days on end, Swanepoel would do his rounds to the various rooms at Compol, to take note of which detainees might be about to break, ready to stick the knife between ribs. The detainees were interrogated in small rooms in the multi-storey building, which were furnished with a desk, chair, bricks and a single blinding light. Windows were boarded up. Trying to extract statements from them, their tormentors resorted to any means. Plucking out moustache hairs, the standing on bricks, days and nights of keeping them awake. One detainee recounted to a journalist:

> Swanepoel did klap (slap) me on my face very hard, changing hands, left, right, left, right, and said, "K***ir, ek sal vir jou wakker maak (I will make you wake up). *Kommunis* (communist), why aren't you frightened?" Now during these four days and three nights on these bricks my feet and legs were swollen, the whole body was numb; I could not walk when I came down from the bricks".[7]

Joyce was of the opinion that the hundreds of detainees would bear the emotional scars of their torture for years and years afterwards. Some of those who survived physically would later commit suicide as a result of what they had shared under duress. She said it was secondary torture post-1994, for those policemen to watch how some political heroes of the time unravelled in the new South Africa.

> It is not only your intellect which is important in your life, it is also emotions, your relationships with other people, how to deal with these people. That is why I am saying that enduring race which I was in, fighting for change in this country, I think, was a price to pay for the separation with my son. I was not going to break down. That is another way they dealt with us.[8]

Of Swanepoel, she wrote:

> He did not stab, he did not put the electrical shocker on, you know, sexual parts of his victims, but he was behind those menials, the men who did that. He was the paymaster of those people. People who fell (off the bricks), it was not just a question of falling and dying at the hands of the enemy, it was also at what they turned you to become later on. Others have become monsters, okay. That is part of falling and that is what the enemy enjoyed and that is what they are enjoying today, people like Johan Coetzee, you know, Swanepoel … ask those people why did they turn people into this. I think they will find the answer there.[9]

Even among the friends, they planted suspicions which would surface years later. In one biography, Winnie Mandela wrote that she believed that Joyce had turned and she tried to send a message to her to be strong, even though this was not true and Joyce had refused to give a statement. Detainees were told of special arrangements made for others – money and food, because they knew their families were starving. Racial antagonisms were inflamed and bribes offered, such as passports and diplomatic posts.

Swanepoel's reign was long and so was his reach. The TRC heard evidence that he was the central figure in the anti-terrorist unit Koevoet, which operated in South West Africa (Namibia), and in 1976, during the Soweto uprising, it was Swanepoel who was called out to Soweto when riots broke out. It was Swanepoel who called for arms.

His testimony, which was read out at the TRC hearings – he did not have the gall to attend in person – gives clues to his malicious mind. He appeared to have suffered no remorse for his deeds.

> By the time we got to Soweto everything was in flames. It was chaos. It was a tragic scene to look at – cars being burnt, people being killed. Everything was chaotic and completely out of control. We had far too few men available for the situation ... Eventually I landed up, after a couple of days, in charge of riots all over Johannesburg – Soweto and Alexandra. I made my mark. I let it be known to the rioters I would not tolerate what was happening. I used appropriate force. In Soweto and Alexandra where I operated, that broke the back of the organisers.

More than 451 schoolchildren were shot and killed by police.

In July 1998, a UK newspaper report recorded that Swanepoel, aged 70, had died "quietly at home."

> Swanepoel lived quietly in retirement on his pension still paid by the Mandela Government in (Roodepoort) an outer suburb of Johannesburg. He made no move to seek amnesty from the Truth and Reconciliation Commission. One of his former victims who wished to bring charges against him discovered however that Swanepoel's career may have taken its toll, for by his sixties he was already suffering from premature senility.[10]

Notes

1 O'Malley, n.d.
2 O'Malley, n.d.
3 IDAF archive.
4 IDAF archive.
5 Du Preez Bezdrob, 2004.
6 Du Preez Bezdrob, 2004.
7 IDAF archive.
8 TRC transcripts.
9 TRC transcripts.
10 *The Times*, London, July 1998.

9   Winnie Madikizela-Mandela

Solitary confinement was designed to kill you so slowly that you were long dead before you died. By the time you died, you were nobody. You had no soul anymore and a body without a soul is a corpse anyway. It is unbelievable that you survived all that. When I was told that most of my torturers were dead, I was so heartbroken. I wanted them to see the dawn of freedom. I wanted them to see how they lost their battle with all that they did to us, that we survived. We are the survivors who made this history. They tortured us knowing that it was going to leak to the country and they wanted to test the reaction.[1]

Winnie Madikizela-Mandela

Being a figurehead for the banned African National Congress (ANC), Winnie Mandela would have been target number one for the apartheid government after the Rivonia triallists were imprisoned. Her role in fuelling the movement with information and discourse, but also courage, pushing the strong men and women – including those in this story – was a threat likened to military warfare. It fell on her shoulders to continue with their work despite the dangers to themselves and their families.

To share with those who could see the big picture, the long game, with penalties like death, harassment, imprisonment and torture was a lot to ask of a young woman, raising young children while her husband was in prison for an indefinite amount of time – she could never have known it would be 27 years.

One of the most significant of the impacts on her and other women was their strained mental capacity. Shanthie Naidoo spoke about how her own mother, Ama, a stalwart in Federation of South African Woman (FEDSAW) and the early days of the resistance campaign, allowed her grandmother to "adopt" her. She was sent to her to live with her cousins in Marabastad, Pretoria, until she was a teenager. "She couldn't cope," Shanthie told me.

Prema was just born and I went to live with my grandmother when I was about thirteen months old. There were five of us children. I was the

DOI: 10.4324/9781003228905-10

eldest, and the only girl, so my grandmother doted on me. It was okay, because it wasn't easy for my mother to take care of everyone.

Ama was responsible for mobilising thousands of women and feeding the Rivonia triallists for over two years, as well as being a homemaker, often as a single parent. Her grandmother wanted to adopt Shanthie so she could keep watch over the precious girl child who was born after many sons in the family. Shanthie would only return home to Doornfontein when she was a teenager.

When the government was not shy physically to stop activists who contributed to the momentum of movement, the modus operandi of the security police was to push the activists towards paranoia, insanity, incapacitation. Spying on their every move, lengthy periods of detention, with solitary confinement the trump card.

Winnie Mandela's home was raided regularly, at any time of the day or night. They would take anything that was precious to her, letters from her husband, birthday cards.

> It means paging through each and every book on your shelves, lifting carpets, looking under beds, lifting sleeping children from mattresses and looking under the sheets. It means tasting your sugar, your mealie-meal and every spice on your kitchen shelf. Unpacking all your clothing and going through each pocket. Ultimately, it means your seizure at dawn, dragged away from little children screaming and clinging to your skirt, imploring the white man dragging Mummy away to leave her alone.[2]

When she was arrested for the longer detention in 1969 in the early hours, her two daughters, Zenani and Zindzi, then ten and nine years old, began to cry in panic, but the police would neither allow her to comfort them nor make arrangements for their care. Ignoring her pleas that she could not leave the children there, unattended, they jostled her to the door, where rough hands prised the screaming children from their mother's side and someone said they would drive them to the home of one of Winnie's sisters. Her daughters' terrified wailing would ring in her ears for months afterwards. Winnie was not yet 35. Nelson Mandela had been on Robben Island for five years.

She was refused permission to contact her lawyer, relatives or friends. She knew that the Terrorism Act meant she could be arrested without a warrant, detained for an indefinite period of time, interrogated and kept in solitary confinement without access to a lawyer or relative.

She was taken to Pretoria and placed in solitary confinement. Winnie didn't know that she was one of 22 people arrested in coordinated countrywide raids at that time.

It is heartening to note how Gillian Slovo recalled her mother, anti-apartheid activist and writer Ruth First's, imprisonment in the 1950s:

> She wrote unflinchingly of the humiliation of being locked away, caught peering in desperation though her own peephole ... about the effects of the loneliness and sensory deprivation that eventually drove her to the brink. The book (*117 Days*) is a serious testimony to the distance apartheid South Africa was prepared to travel in order to stop a woman like Ruth who had chosen to keep her conscience clean in a society riddled with guilt.[3]

First wrote: "There was only one way out, before I drove myself mad ... I reached for the phial of pills and swallowed the lot."[4] She was unsuccessful in her attempt to end her life.

Meanwhile, the prison conditions of black women tell a different story from those of white women. For instance in *117 Days*, Ruth First described how she had a desk to sit at, passable ablution facilities and books.

In contrast, the diaries from Winnie Mandela's detention, found about 40 years later, describe how she, too, contemplated suicide soon after being detained because of the stark circumstances. In addition to using a galvanised bucket as a toilet, she had to wash over it with a little water from her 1-litre ration. As a person who was fastidious about cleanliness, she had to spare water for drinking, and for washing she would pour a little water onto her hands and vigorously rub her hands and face, then use her underwear to sponge her body.

> During the second week of April I just could not take solitary confinement any more. I realised it might go on for another year before we were charged. There was no sign that we were going to be interrogated again.
>
> It suddenly dawned on me that if I took my life there would be no trial and my colleagues would be saved from the tortuous mental agony of solitary confinement. The long and empty hours tore through the inner core of my soul. There were moments when I got so fed up I banged my head against the cell wall. Physical pain was more tolerable. I decided I would commit suicide but would do so gradually so that I should die of natural causes to spare Nelson and the children the pain of knowing I had taken my life.[5]

There is little doubt that interrogation and torture techniques made Winnie gravely ill. The most intense session lasted five days. She was not allowed to sleep. They taunted her, saying that they would display her around the world as the woman who could stay awake the longest of them all. Because she had an existing heart condition, she was allowed to sit down while security branch operatives questioned her. Her body became swollen and blue.

She was not beaten, however, possibly because the international press was watching the government's treatment of her as best as they could. All eyes would be on her in a pending trial. They reminded her that she had brought herself to prison, and likewise she could release herself. Swanepoel said:

> You also wanted to pretend you're a leader; and you're nothing, Winnie Mandela, we mean to prove to the world your worth. You are just fit for a kick in the backside. What did you drag all this scum into politics for?[6]

Instead of blows, it was sleep deprivation and mind games that were meted out to her. First, the security branch officers tried to convince her they had more information on her than they actually did. Her plans were obvious, they said; all she needed to do was put it down in a written statement. "We are giving you a chance to help yourself and your girls," the soft cop said. "Why go through this hardship?" She was young and beautiful, one of her interrogators, Major Coetzee, pointed out to her, and she owed it to Zenani and Zindzi to live a normal life. This tactic, of reminding her of her children and using them as a tool, might have been easier than physical pain. Winnie's heart was breaking for her daughters, from the agony of not knowing what had happened to them – and they knew this. But she remained firm, refusing to crumble. Instead, she retreated into her mind. She would block out the present by going back to the ancestral lands of her childhood, as a daughter of a Pondo chief.

Only one police officer allowed her to put her head between her knees when the blackouts got worse. The others continued to bang the table and clap. The noises from somewhere else in the building continued. The officers would torment her further by telling her that the noises were her comrades who were being "worked on".

> My clothes were soaking wet from excessive night sweating. The bodice was very tight due to oedema (swelling and water retention). I realised my failing health was to their advantage, because if the heart stopped suddenly the interrogators would say I died of natural causes. They seemed quite pleased about it and would ask if my heart had not stopped yet, each time they changed shifts. They refused to give me their names when I asked for them. Two teams would refer to me as "office inventory" asking, "Is office inventory still there?" I was called other names.[7]

When she said she was feeling faint and experiencing severe palpitations, her interrogators promised a doctor if she would decode letters they said they had in evidence. Biographer Anné Mariè Du Preez Bezdrob wrote:

> If she was smart and helped them, they would make life easier for her. Winnie would not even contemplate the idea, and scoffed at his mention of the non-existent, coded letters. Even in her current dire straits, she

could see through his absurd lies. She was exhausted and in pain, but they could forget it – she was getting out of there, even if only in her mind. She was going to go to Pondoland, to its soft green fields in summer, to the voices of the boys as they run and laugh and fight ...[8]

They offered her safekeeping, money. They even tried to convince her to turncoat, and work for the government. Then they turned the assault towards her self-esteem. She was doing her work for fame and wealth, implicating poor people with her lies and her ambitious, troublesome aims.

Swanepoel offered her a cigarette even though he knew she didn't smoke. He offered her coffee and, without even waiting for a response, instructed one of the policemen, in Afrikaans, to get her some. Then, suddenly switching to English, he added that the policeman should get "Mrs Mandela some toasted chicken sandwiches".

If she cooperated and recorded a radio broadcast calling upon ANC forces on the country's borders to lay down their arms and start talking to the government, she would be released. Moreover, she would be flown by helicopter to see Nelson on Robben Island, and he would be moved to the cottage where Robert Sobukwe had been held, so that he could hold secret talks with high-ranking police officers. Winnie was appalled.

> She would never become one of them. How could they think, even for a second, that she could become one of them? In his soothing voice, the good cop (Coetzee) urged her to think about his proposal – then all her problems could soon be over. Winnie willed herself to remember Madiba's voice, planning a holiday in Durban, images of the waltzing waves, the sun bouncing off the water, Zeni and Zindzi building sand castles on the beach ...,[9] wrote Du Preez Bezdrob.

When she fell asleep, they woke her up roughly. Her head was spinning, she was dizzy and disoriented. "At times my mind became totally blank, I could not remember things I had known quite well before. I would take long to register questions. The oedema was at its worst."[10]

One of the officers offered her a shower. As she walked with heavy feet, she felt close to death, exhaustion overcoming her at each step. But once the icy water cascaded over her, new resolve would come through her scrubbed skin.

She reminded herself of the truth. She had no money that they spoke of, and had struggled to maintain her household by herself and with help from the community. Comrades donated food and helped to keep her children in school. Yes, she was dressed decently. It was for her spirit more than anything, but so much of what she owned were gifts from the women who rallied around her.

They continued the interrogation for hours and days, trying to fill in the blanks in their files, piecing together meetings with comrades and uninvolved visitors alike, everyone who had passed through or by her house. They recorded actual movements and meetings, along with the inconsequential: an overseas guest spending the night, visits by women, well-wishers, who knew how tough the days were, to drop off donated clothing for her – the so-called "fashionable" items she was supposedly spending money on.

By the fourth day of Winnie's interrogation, there was blood in her urine. Her body shivered involuntarily and there was a stabbing pain below her left breast. She passed out several times, dreaming of her girls.

Another accusation was one of infidelity, claiming that she was involved with many men while her husband was in prison. They would tell the ANC that she had turned rogue. Nobody would trust her.

And again the banging on the table to keep her awake like a shock to her weary mind.

On the fifth day, it was the turn of the torturer fashioned as the good cop, Major Coetzee. He came to tell her that he was so worried about her that he had not slept for three nights; his wife was worried about his wellbeing as well as his "work". He called the interrogators in, and they made her aware that they were going to consult in an adjoining office. "By then I was trembling badly and could not control the muscle spasms. The pain under the left breast was acute and I had difficulty in breathing,"[11] she wrote. Then, suddenly, she heard shrieks from the next room. The officers came back in. "Your brave soldiers," they said. They let her hear them without interruption. She thought of her younger sister, who has been detained, and her friends. She couldn't be sure who was being hurt, but it broke her.

That afternoon, Swanepoel returned.

> I told him that if this is what my people were going through, those involved and those innocent ones, then I request that I be allowed to accept the responsibility of each and every one of their actions and that I be charged, that they be used as state witnesses, those who were prepared to give evidence.[12]

She was told she would have to reply to all the questions they wished to confirm before they decided whether there would be any case.

> I told him I confirmed everything that those detained had said, and I was entirely responsible for all they did. I was then flooded with so many questions at a time I could not cope without resting in between. I said "yes" to everything they said. The history they wanted from me dated from my primary school days, high school, how I came to Johannesburg.[13]

Finally, she relented, saying she would cooperate but begging them to release the others.

The interrogation team would have celebrated. But for Winnie, it was a defeat.

While it was a human moment of giving up for the greater good, and she had not admitted to anything particularly incriminating apart from what they already knew, she questioned her actions. As a movement, the comrades should have borne the brunt of their own actions, the consequences of which they were well aware. They stood together and knew the risks. But she was a mortal, a woman and mother who couldn't bear to hear pain inflicted on another human being, no matter what the cause.

All the interrogators and other policemen bombarded her with statements, from reams of papers, asking for her agreement. In her drowsy state she responded in monosyllables. She admitted to calling meetings, writing and sending letters. One pile of letters was from a "friend" she worked out had been an informant, Maud Katzenellenbogen. She was asked to explain the coded messages and admit to what was in her handwriting. "They seemed to know the name of every person to whom she had ever written," Du Preez Bezdrob wrote.

> The interrogation went on for hours until, finally, the chief interrogator, Swanepoel, said it was enough, they had what they needed, and Winnie was returned to her cell. After being awake for five days and five nights, she could not go to sleep, and lay there for some time, muttering incoherently.
>
> I am in the cell again. How did I get here. I can't sleep but I am so, so tired. They send food with the toilet bucket. It must be poisoned. I can't touch it.[14]

After the ordeal, she had terrible stomach cramps and was sick in her galvanised bucket. When sleep finally came, it was interrupted, fitful, the screams from her nightmares waking her.

The team would have brought her back to the cell during a blackout. In the quiet again, she had to push the interrogation out of her mind, or it would have succeeded in its purpose. She tore one of the blankets to shreds, then wove the threads together as her grandmother had taught her to do when she was a child, making traditional mats with a grass called *uluzi*. For days she knitted the strands together, undid them, wove them together again.

Slowly, "normality" returned to the cell. It was just a few weeks into the detention, but she was filled with rage at the treatment and experience.

Memoirs recount how she would look for insects in her cell. A social, busy activist now had precious ants for companions. That, too, was not allowed once the prison officials got wind of it. After she spent a day playing with the ants on her hands, a wardress noticed, scolded her and switched off the light. Back into darkness. On some days the bright light would stay on indefinitely, adding to her insomnia.

She was given a respite of sorts – a Bible, which the warder threw onto the floor with contempt, suggesting she pray hard for her release. They demanded she pray in isiXhosa, not English. Later she would notice the anger in her captors if she spoke English. Major Swanepoel was enraged when she answered him in English, apparently because he couldn't fully understand it. There was some common ground, then, in language battles. For both, the language issue was a touchy subject. Both sides had fought battles around language in South Africa, and the tension around choice of language reared an ugly head when it came up in the prisons.

Meanwhile, the Bible became a companion and voice of both comfort and discomfort, read and re-read for what would be close to two years. She would later say that some days it gave her peace, and on other days she became despondent and the words felt meaningless in light of her situation.

The treatment of political prisoners became more inhumane as their trial date neared. In July, Swanepoel walked into her cell and demanded to know who Thembi Mandela was. This was Nelson Mandela's son, her stepson, she told him. "Well, he is dead, he was killed in a car accident," Swanepoel said, turning on his heel. The mourning was immediate and profound. She wailed and wept inconsolably – not that there was anyone who could comfort her.

Thembi was just 19, and close to Madiba's heart. He had promised to care for the family in his father's absence. And now he was gone. She mourned alone, for her husband who was either unaware or mourning by himself 1,500 km away on his prison island. And she mourned for both their situations. Sadness filled her tiny, grey space, and it permeated throughout the prison population.

For one, the callousness of the security police was reiterated to them all, and the disregard for mourning, tragedy, their lives evident. Hatred would grow in their hearts for those who could be so cruel and cold.

The women had to rally together in some way, since physical closeness was not possible. Word of Thembi's death spread through the cells. Being innovative in the time of isolation with little means of communicating, the women managed to pass Winnie a letter – via her toilet bucket. Likely the only space that wasn't watched closely by the prison warders, the galvanised bucket was brought in by a prisoner and accompanied by food. On a particular day, Winnie lifted the plate and a flash of silver caught her eye at the bucket. Wrapped in the silver paper was a note of commiseration from other prisoners, expressing their sympathy about Thembi's death. The last sentence read: "Mother of the Nation, we are with you." Her return mail on the silver paper was written with a piece of a pin.

Another message came, this one wrapped in a banana skin. It was a warning, an incorrect one, saying that Joyce Sikhakhane had been broken from excessive interrogation. She was being transferred to Barberton in Mpumalanga or Nylstroom prison in Limpopo where they would take her statement to be used in testimony against the 22. Using the shard of pin, Winnie scratched a message on the banana skin: "Joyce, don't you dare." She needn't have worried about the message getting to Joyce, because it was that decade's version of fake news, which travelled just as quickly as it does in current times.

Singing was another form of communication, especially when in the languages unfamiliar to the warders. One day, after months of silence, Winnie heard a woman singing in isiXhosa from a nearby cell. *Igama lam ndinguNondwe.* "My name is Nondwe," she sang, sending a message that she was there, and alive. Nondwe shared that she had been caught in Port Elizabeth and when she had been detained. Winnie also shared news, that two comrades they knew in common had been killed in detention.

Finally, in August 1969, the first court appearance was upon the 22 detainees. Well-known human rights lawyer and Mandela family friend Joel Carlson was asked to represent the triallists. Carlson's anti-apartheid stance was known. Swanepoel tried to intervene with a lawyer of the state's choice, Mendel Levin. Swift arrangements were made for Winnie to convince the other accused to accept the tainted counsel. Swanepoel had been confident that Levin would quickly wrap up the case and imprison his detainees. Lawrence and Rita Ndzanga and another triallist, Elliot Shabangu, also testified that the security police had tried to coerce them into accepting Levin as their attorney – Swanepoel had claimed that Carlson was not available.

However, it was the ally, Carlson, who turned up in court and told the judge that Nelson Mandela had engaged him to defend the triallists. However, he had been denied access to Winnie and the other accused, whose relatives had also engaged his services.

Carlson included George Bizos and Arthur Chaskalson, who had defended Nelson Mandela during the Rivonia Trial, in the defence team. Somehow, long distance attempts to help the 22 had come to fruition. Bizos immediately obtained a court order giving all the accused access to basic ablution facilities, and Winnie was finally able to take a proper shower after six months.

They didn't relent entirely, despite the triallists now being covered by legal counsel who watched over them and monitored their condition. Returning to her cell after consulting with her legal team one day, Winnie found her clothes strewn on the floor, covered in her new hand and face cream and trampled by muddy shoes. She had no way of washing or ironing her clothes.

By now she was also suffering from malnutrition and showed the typical symptoms: pallid complexion, skin sores and bleeding gums. She had developed regular fevers and continued to suffer periodic blackouts. Finally, she was admitted to the prison hospital.

When the second trial began in October, Winnie was in hospital, running a high fever.

In December when the case reconvened, she was still unwell but was strong enough during proceedings. Asked to plead, she made a statement, saying that she had been held in detention for months, in terms of a law she regarded as "unjust and immoral, and which had claimed the life of one of her colleagues, Caleb Mayekiso, who had died in detention three weeks after the arrests."[15]

Justice Bekker insisted that she enter a plea, but she said she found it difficult to do so, as she felt that she had already been found guilty.

The defence team drew the court's attention to the fact that all but 12 of the 540 charges in the indictment were identical to those withdrawn by the prosecution during the earlier trial. They began laboriously reading out the two indictments, word for word, to illustrate their argument.

The police action had also caused an outcry despite the government ignoring all criticism, the international legal teams noted. The relatives of 15 detainees had applied unsuccessfully for a court order restraining the security police from torturing them, and widespread protests were staged outside the Old Synagogue.

The case was disintegrating and the evidence was found to be as flimsy as the clothing some of the triallists were still wearing after more than a year in prison. On the third day of the trial, the judge halted proceedings and acquitted the accused, without a single witness being called.

Despite the case being dismissed again, they were again held under the 90-day detention laws. In June 1970, formal charges were dropped against the accused. This time, they really were free to go home.

Winnie immediately thought of sending telegrams to Robben Island and to her children, who were by then in Swaziland, to tell them she was free. Back at home in Soweto, she took some time to readjust to the normal rhythms of the day, after what would be the worst months of her life.

For a long while, she did not feel that she was safe or truly free to move around. She was obviously emotionally scarred, but also showed physical evidence of the experience. Her skin was blotchy with the unmistakable signs of vitamin deficiency, and it was a slow process to regain her health and self-confidence. To top it all, she was served with a five-year banning order just as she was about to leave on a journey to visit her husband in prison in the Western Cape after two years.

The detention, banning and surveillance didn't stop her from continuing her work. She gave interviews to the international press, saying she would not be intimidated. In May 1973 Winnie was arrested again for meeting with her friend and detainee in the 1969 trial, Peter Magubane. She served six months in prison in Kroonstad's women's jail, which was far more hospitable than her previous detention.

The mid-1970s saw the country in a state of unrest. The Black Consciousness Movement and student uprisings which began on the morning of 16 June 1976 were in full force. She became a symbol for the students who were protesting against Afrikaans being used as a medium of instruction in schools.

She established a parents' movement in Soweto to help parents of students who were arrested and detained. When the security police looked for instigators of the 1976 uprising, she again took the fall and was held in custody for five months; she was released in December 1976 without charge. Her new banning order arrived in January 1977 ... another five years of restricted movement.

Then, one morning in May 1977, they stormed into her house again. Her belongings were thrown together and she was told she was being moved. Crockery, books, clothing were bundled in blankets. With her daughter, Zindizi, who was 16, she was banished to a three-bedroomed ramshackle house without running water in the Free State town of Brandfort, about 50 km from Bloemfontein.

There she was regarded as an alien by the small community. They knew her only as Nelson's wife. She said

> I have ceased a long time ago, to exist as an individual. The ideals, the political goals that I stand for, these are the ideals and goals of the people in this country. My private self doesn't exist. Whatever they do to me, they do to the people of this country. What I stand for is what they want to banish. I couldn't think of a greater honour,[16]

True to form, Winnie did not stop working. She established a clinic, a crèche and a women's movement in her meagre surroundings in the dusty town where poverty and malnutrition were as rife as the blatant racism they experienced. She lived there for four years.

****

Du Preez Bezdrob wrote in her biography of Winnie Mandela in 2004 that it has "been speculated that like so many South Africans traumatised by the brutality of life under apartheid, Winnie may have long suffered from Post-Traumatic Stress Disorder and her actions ought to be understood in light of this."[17]

A documentary film, *Winnie*, by Pascale Lamche, released after her death gave insight into disputed narratives. The summary describes the alternative story.

> Winnie Madikizela-Mandela is one of the most misunderstood and intriguingly powerful contemporary female political figures. Her rise and seeming fall from grace bear the hallmarks of epic tragedy. For the first time, this film pieces together and properly considers her life and contribution to the struggle to bring down apartheid from the inside, with intimate insight from those who were closest to her and with testimony from the enemies who sought to extinguish her radical capacity to shake up the order of things.
>
> Supremely controversial, Winnie is routinely represented as victim turned perpetrator. Her repeated demonisation in the media has been amplified abroad to such a degree that the passionate respect she elicits among those who still struggle in South Africa, seems a paradox. And that's what intrigues us. How did this occur and more importantly, to what ends?[18]

There is no doubt that there were many sides to Winnie Mandela, which eventually saw her estranged from some of her closest friends and comrades, including elders like Albertina Sisulu and her own husband. Towards the end of her life, she fell out of the ANC structures too.

It is important to consider the whole person and what led to shaping her character after imprisonment and banishment. We know that political prisoners had been severely beaten, shocked with electrical wires and endured other forms of torture. But the worst recorded result comes from solitary confinement.

Nelson Mandela, who had been imprisoned in harsh conditions and forced to perform years of hard labour on Robben Island, said he had found his own brief encounter with solitary confinement – three days – "the most forbidding aspect of prison life." Winnie Mandela was in solitary confinement for 18 months.

Notes

1 Madikizela-Mandela, 2013.
2 Madikizela-Mandela, 2013.
3 First, 1965.
4 First, 1965.
5 Madikizela-Mandela, 2013.
6 Du Preez Bezdrob, 2004.
7 Du Preez Bezdrob, 2004.
8 Du Preez Bezdrob, 2004.
9 Du Preez Bezdrob, 2004.
10 Du Preez Bezdrob, 2004.
11 Mandela, 2013.
12 Mandela, 2013.
13 Mandela, 2013.
14 Du Preez Bezdrob, 2004.
15 Du Preez Bezdrob, 2004.
16 Madikizela-Mandela, 1984.
17 Du Preez Bezdrob, 2004.
18 Lamche, 2018.

10 Aftermath

The children were thrown in the streets to fend for themselves. Some swelled the ranks of the liberation movement, the unlucky ones turned tsotsis (criminals).

Joyce Sikhakhane-Rankin

A significant question in the conversations I had with the four women – Joyce Sikhakhane-Rankin, Shanthie Naidoo, Rita Ndzanga and Nondwe Mankahla – was around their mental wellbeing and the effects of detention on their lives, but this went beyond them as individuals. While they themselves do not show obvious injuries and scars, and say they have recovered reasonably well from the mental assault, the impact on their children and loved ones is undeniable.

This impact was not always negative. There were definite, generational effects from their detention and contribution to the cause which inspired some. Each of their families is incredibly proud of the sacrifices the women made, which was for the individual good as much as it was for the country. However, for some, the sacrifice will be projected forward in this way. There were children who still bear the invisible scars from their formative years.

Phila Mankhala lives with her mother, Nondwe, in their New Brighton home. She is in her 50s, unemployed because of an epileptic condition. She says it took decades for her to recognise Nondwe as her mother.

> I was about ten years old when my mum was in prison for a long time, but she was in and out (of our lives) for years before. I didn't know her very well. We were raised by my grandmother. Sometimes, I used to ask Granny, "Where is the person we called Mama?" but otherwise we just carried on. We were a big family so maybe we didn't notice too much. There are four of us siblings, and Mum's sister had her own children. My grandmother, Nellie, was there … she really did a lot for us.

Phila says even when her mother wasn't detained, Nondwe's activities kept her away from home when they were young. "I know when she wasn't around

DOI: 10.4324/9781003228905-11

the special branch used to come home and look for her. They were in plain-clothes in a nice car, not a police car," she says. "What usually happened when Mum was not around was *amalady* as we called them, social workers, would come check on us and bring us food."

The adjustment after her long detention in 1969 was tough, because Nondwe was banned and spent more time at home than she had for a long time.

Phila remembers her arriving from Pretoria after the detention.

> When Mum came back, *sjoe*, I didn't know her. I didn't remember this person. She could have been anyone. We were not close, and in fact we fought a lot because she was distant at first, but she was also strict. Even simple things like asking when I needed something, I would ask my granny for many years, not Mum. It wasn't until I went to college that I tried to have a relationship with her. It took all that time to develop a relationship again.

As an adult, Phila worked with African National Congress (ANC) stalwart Govan Mbeki for a time.

> That was when I grew up and finally I understood why she went away, why she wasn't at home. We really didn't know as kids. It helped me to understand, and it was a good reason for her to (get involved). If it was me, I would do the same.

Phila pauses, then adds, "But maybe, at least if we were a bit older, it would have been different." She doesn't elaborate, saying only that her mother "did a lot for this country."

"It was important for her and the others to fight for the country. It did hurt us as children, we missed her, and we were young. But I am still so proud of her."

Nondwe's elder daughter, Nombuso, died from alcoholism-related illness. The remaining family is scattered around the country, but they are as functional as can be expected. Phila says,

> Now we are close again but my youngest sister, I don't think they will be close. We try to talk about it and explain what was going on. She has no interest even in hearing what happened and why Mum went away.

The extended family went through financial hardship, a familiar scenario for many detainees, veterans and those who chose to get involved in the movement. "I'm not sure if we saw the benefits of it. There are rewards which people speak about, but working for your country ... there is no need for reward. We know we were also a part of the people in the country, so we all benefited in that way," says Phila.

She adds that people still come to the house to ask for advice and help in the community.

> From time to time, people who need knowledge from her will visit us. Not many young people though. They should hear her story. She's 85 now, and for her to be in this position where she is, still working and a sort of active politician at her age ... I wish she can rest a little and sit down more.

****

Laurette Ndzanga, Ma Rita's granddaughter, says she can't bear to hear the stories of her grandmother's detention.

> It is hard watching her get so frail knowing how strong she used to be. I'm grateful to be living off the fruits of her and others' labour but when I see what goes on in our democracy, it is hurtful. For me, the only way to stay on track and grow in the country is to remember their contribution, especially in tough times.

The tall young woman with a bright smile that sometimes disappears when she's asked questions about the family's experience says she was born in exile. "My mum, Thami, was in exile in Germany and I was born in Potsdam," she says. They moved from the castled city on the border of Berlin to Soweto in 1991. 'We would visit South Africa when we could – I remember coming to Johannesburg as a nine year old – but I always wanted to come home. I felt connected to South Africa even though I wasn't born here. And you know when you are just a little different, when you live in a place like Germany. Being away, means even hearing people say your African name properly is something unusual', she says of her first name, Nonkululeko.

She and her mother lived in Tanzania, Zambia and the UK before she moved back permanently. Even though she hadn't visited often, Soweto "felt like home, because for me it was about seeing my family. There were no cousins or uncles in Germany."

Her uncle, Ma Rita's youngest son Cecil, remembers a lot of the stories from his childhood.

> My dad was the head of the house, and he would always call his kids and say this is how things are done, and this is what we need to do. When my parents were in prison, we just got by. Mum says how we would have black tea sometimes, but if comrades needed help we would buy food, even pap and spinach from the garden. We grew up that way. There were lots of horrible, horrible things done to us by the special branch and by other people, but it didn't stop us. Even when my father died, Mum continued. As a young boy I used to see a lot of people coming in and

out at our family home in Soweto. I got used to them as they visited our home regularly and our parents introduced us to them as Mr Poloto, Mrs Mandela and others.

When the house was raided in 1969, Cecil was about nine years old. He says

That event made me aware of the political activities that were taking place at home and I started understanding that all the time these were secret meetings being held in the house. And that's how we got involved as children. We would be on the lookout for the special branch who constantly monitored our home. We knew to get legal representation for our parents when they got detained. When they were out of prison, our parents then started informing us about their activities and that we were not to tell anyone about what took place at home.

Not only meetings were held at our home. My parents were also recruiting for the ANC, which was banned during those years, and maintained contact and communication with the ANC in exile, including distributing political literature. To curtail these activities, the government of the time decided to ban my parents and other people. That meant they were not to leave their house, not to have visitors, and not to work in Johannesburg. They had to report time and again at Moroka police station.

Despite the banning order, his parents continued their work but they went underground. "It did affect us, so much, now and back then. We were not with our parents, which I think hardened us.

In 1977, when my father died in detention ... this hurt us a family, since he was a central figure who held the family together, despite the difficulties we were in. I was devastated and ended up not doing well in school although I was one of the better scholars in class. It affected my life as a kid growing up not having him a figurehead. We had no counselling but at the time, it was relatives who consoled us. As they always say, the movement was our family too, says Cecil."

****

Nomzamo Rankin was the seven-month-old baby Joyce left behind when she went into exile in 1972. Now 47, she says,

I don't really remember much of her being away, but I do remember my grandmother used to look after us when we lived in Soweto. When we moved to Scotland, I was about four years old and my older brother, Oliver (Nkosinathi), about eleven. We travelled with my grandmother, Amelia, in 1977 because it was becoming impossible in South Africa around the time of the Soweto uprisings. We met with our other brothers (Vikela, Samora and Allan), Dad and Mum. It was a good time.

Nomzamo is a development economist and she lives in Sheffield in South Yorkshire. Scotland was idyllic, she remembers. "We had a good upbringing in Dundee and our parents really cherished us as children. We didn't have any hardships, really. I remember playing a lot, cycling down one of the roads and having races. We also had new grandparents who were there, from my dad's side," she says, referring to Ken Rankin's parents.

She says her mother didn't speak of her detention and exile much when they were children; instead, she talked more about how much she looked forward to having the children together. "We were quite close growing up even though our formative years were spent differently. We understood why our upbringings were different," Nomzamo says, including her half-siblings and adopted brother, Vikela, in this. Joyce and Ken did tell the kids about South Africa, though.

> I know we met Aunty Shanthie, who was in exile in the UK. She and Mum kept in touch and their paths would cross now and then. I do know about it now, and it was a difficult time in their political work when they were in prison. She sacrificed a lot of the time with the family for the greater good. It is admirable that she was one of the people in the forefront of the fight against apartheid.

As the only daughter, Nomzamo says she finds the work her mother did out of the ordinary, especially for a woman of that era.

> In terms of my mum's contribution, I admire her spirit. It's not easy to sacrifice your career and your children for your country. She was important and special and the history should be shared to know what commitment it takes to transform a country.

Nomzamo spent much of her adulthood in South Africa.

> I definitely thought of South Africa as a special place, if only for the fact that there were people who committed themselves to free the people of apartheid … I always grew up knowing it is special. Maybe part of that was wanting to go and visit, even though we weren't able to. When we came back, it was an adjustment. The romanticism was still there and I was able to find a job easily. We basically got on with life in SA. We were happy to be there but –, she says.

It seems a contradiction hangs in the air. "The but," Nomzamo continues,

> from my point of view, was that there was a sense of alienation. When we were in Scotland, we knew we also had another home but that we couldn't live there because of Mum's political work and what was going on there. So in that sense, we missed a part of our childhood, growing up in other countries rather than our home country, despite the circumstances in South Africa.
>
> Then, when we eventually moved back, we knew we were welcomed back home in SA, and in other African countries that we lived. Even though we feel we are South African, we aren't completely South African because of our history. So wherever we went, I felt more an international citizen. Sometimes being able to relate to people who have never been out of the country or lived elsewhere was not easy. There are gaps of our history and differences in their history, so we welcomed meeting kids who were in exile because there was common ground.

After 25 years, Nomzamo left South Africa to pursue her career in England.

> It's unfortunate that I had to leave but also understandable because of difficult economic times. It is tough times globally, and it is good, in a way, to know that we aren't the only place in the world facing this. The economic development is a result of South Africa's history, yes, but we also can't blame all of it on our problems. Everyone contributed as much as they could. Even Mum had to make her living and build South Africa through her work. She always wanted to be someone who was employed rather than pursuing civil work.

That the children of political activists were deeply, adversely affected in different ways during the apartheid era, perhaps more especially those whose parents suffered or died in detention, should never be refuted. It is a common thread among that generation.

The effect on Oliver Nkosinathi Rankin, Joyce's son, who was 54 at the time of writing, was profound. From his home in Huddersfield, West Yorkshire, he shares with me that this is one of the first times he has been interviewed about his experience in relation to his mother.

As an adult in his 20s he attended Joyce's Truth and Reconciliation Commission (TRC) hearing.

> I remember I cried for days after the hearing because of what she had gone through. After that I employed the coping mechanism which I have used most of my life, I now realise: forgetting about it and not thinking about it. I left it to my parents, hoping that one day they would sit down and explain. I think they both found it hard, and to this day that has not happened. Most of the things that Mum went through I

learned through other people or from what I have read. Not from her. It has affected me.

The thoughts seem to spill out of his mind. His story is one that is inextricably tied to South Africa, even though he was moved around the world by his parents in their commitment to the liberation of the country at the bottom of the African continent.

"When I was in South Africa during 2017, I attended a life coaching course and what emanated from this was that I realised I had never dealt with the unique way I grew up," he tells me.

> I have always trusted the decisions I have made because I became self-reliant at an early age and therefore any decisions I made only impacted on me; whether right or wrong. Then I got married at 22 and was a dad at 23. This was the first time I became responsible for others. I have to say now, in retrospect, I thought I managed it reasonably, because my family was supported really well. However, I did frequently have bouts of anxiety and depression arising from not knowing why my mother had chosen to "abandon" me at that young age. She was in her early 20s when she was deeply involved with the ANC. To this day I have never blamed her for it. She had to do what she had to do.

However, as a seven-year-old, he was left with his grandmother until Joyce could bring the children together again. He was 11 when he was uplifted from his home in Soweto to move to Dundee in Scotland, then uprooted again once he had settled there, to Mozambique, then to Swaziland, Zimbabwe and finally South Africa. His life has been a series of journeys.

He only vaguely remembers the journey to the UK in 1977.

I didn't know what was happening. At the time living in Soweto, the matriarch was my grandmother, Amelia. It was during the uprisings and she protected me from things that were going on. I wasn't aware at all that my mother had gone into exile.

> I remember the day when were in Jan Smuts Airport, boarding the plane to go to the UK. I remember us boarding the plane with Nana (his sister Nomzamo), two other people whom I don't remember clearly, and my grandmother. I later learned the story of how we could go over. Mum and Dad were able to get politicians in London, Labour Party minister Robin Cook, in particular, who was able to get us over by putting political pressure on the South African government. We didn't have passports and hadn't been out of the country.
>
> I don't know if it was exciting, but as an eleven year old out of Johannesburg who had never travelled overseas, it was a milestone. I remember the flight, and landing in Heathrow, mostly because of the change in temperature. I must have fallen asleep because I remember waking

up when we were landing, and feeling the cold. When the plane was descending, I remember us going through the clouds and then being met at the airport by Mum and Dad and my other siblings.

He describes himself as a reserved person.

As a boy, I was not very emotional. I remember being happy to see Mum but I didn't have a sense of a time since I'd last seen her ... of missing her. It was more a feeling of recognition: Oh, there's Mum. Growing up in Soweto, I hardly saw her anyway. She was a young mother and working, and very involved in her political work. In terms of being a motherly presence, she wasn't there, which is not a criticism, it is just how it was. We always had the support of my grandmother.

At first they stayed with friends in London's Muswell Hill. "It wasn't such an adjustment for me, surprisingly, but I know that suddenly there were many more white people," he laughs.

But it didn't register much and I know some of our ANC kids who actually were traumatised by the place because it was so different. It wasn't like that for me. I realise, now, that it was part of my coping mechanism, to register and then disregard sudden changes like that.

The family travelled to Scotland which would become their new home.

When I saw Vikela for the first time, we were close in age and there was an immediate acceptance, I didn't question it. We were in Edinburgh to meet the new extended family. My dad's parents and uncles and aunts added a lot to our lives, it was really good. And then we moved to Dundee, that is where we were based. And that's where I started school properly.

Nkosinathi says his schooling was interrupted by South Africa's instability.
   To be truthful, I didn't really go to school before moving to the UK. I know we tried. There was a specific date, June 16, 1976, when I was ten years old. [The Soweto uprisings, a series of demonstrations and protests led by black school children in South Africa against inferior state education took place on this day. At least 176 children were killed.] That was my first day in class. Of course, half an hour later we were told to get out of class – and I never went back.
   He gives a wry laugh as he recounts this, then continues:

So, I hadn't gone to school until we moved to Scotland in 1977. I can't explain how I caught up. I could read, I knew how to write, and do maths. I don't have any clear recall of how that came to be. The only thing I can think of is that my grandmother taught me.

His grandmother returned to South Africa where, in the 1980s, she passed away. "We were overseas when my grandmother died," Nkosinathi says. "In fact, I haven't visited her grave."

He remembers being enrolled in school and that he was the first black person to attend the primary school in Dundee. "The school was called Blackness Primary, ironically," he says. "I was put in a class with kids my same age, and mostly, I fitted in. Again, with my coping mechanism, I didn't realise I was the only black person in a school of white children."

He does recall one incident around the American television series *Roots*, which is about a Gambian slave's journey into America. "There was a boy called Frankie who had watched this show and was very fascinated with the main character, Kunta Kinte, and how he looked like me. And of course, Frankie would call me Kunta Kinte," he says with slight chagrin. "I didn't know, but people around me made me realise it was a racist term. I don't think Frankie knew either, and we actually became really good friends after we worked that out."

Life progressed steadily ... but it wasn't going to remain still for long. "I got promoted a year forward," Nkosinathi says, "and moved to high school. Then, in my first year in high school, Mum and Dad suddenly threw a bombshell – we were moving to Mozambique!" He laughs.

> We packed up quite quickly. They were obviously planning it, but for us kids it was sudden. We ended up in Maputo, and that wasn't a very nice experience for me. We had no worries in Scotland, we could get everything we needed, our friends were there, and we had shops and cinemas. Well, we arrived at the airport and as soon as I got off the plane I got a nosebleed – because it was so hot.

Memories that come back include living in a substandard hotel "in the middle of nowhere" where his father contracted a furious bout of food poisoning.

> That prompted my mother to take us four children straight to the housing department. She said, "We are not leaving until you find us a place to stay" and basically barricaded ourselves at the ministry. That night they found us a place to go to ... a house barely furnished and not nice at all. I had gone up the stairs to the bathroom, the water from the tap was brown and the pipes made a huge banging noise.

After a few weeks, the family eventually settled in a proper house close to the beach. The children were enrolled in the international school with children of diplomats and foreign workers like his father. "There were friends from the UK, Holland and China etcetera."

But once again he was jarred from his idyll. "Suddenly I was told that I, only I, would be moved to Swaziland to attend boarding school."

The teenager was not thrilled at the idea, but accepted the change with his father's encouragement.

Everything for me wasn't permanent. Dad just said, "Let's pack," one weekend. So Maputo to Manzini happened really quickly. I only found out much, much later, and maybe I should have known, that the choice of Mozambique was because they (his parents) were very much involved in the ANC movement, which was quite active in Swaziland. I lived in a flat alone with a helper, and went to school. There I became good friends with Helena Dolny (who would later be married to ANC leader Joe Slovo). I spent a lot of time with Auntie Ruth (First), and we sometimes saw Auntie Shanthie, and Uncle Joe. But I didn't know them as part of the movement. They were our friends and family.

A random thought comes to him while thinking about his high school days.

There were South African prisoners in Swaziland, and the police station cells were on my school route. In fact my uncle was once imprisoned there for a while and he could see me from the road. I would try and walk past at the same time all the time, to create a routine so that we could greet each other.

He went to a Catholic school, Salesian High School. He says

There I was, this young guy with a Scottish accent, I might have been fourteen, and I got put in a class which they said was on my level. But the class was with 19, 20 and 21 year olds. They were scary big guys with beards and deep voices.

"Of course, that meant I grew up very quickly."
 He also experienced the direct effects of the armed struggle building up across the border from his home country. "I was back in Mozambique during the school holidays and we heard that the area I stayed in in Swaziland was bombed. A lot of cadres died in the attack."
 He later discovered another reason that the family needed a connection between the two countries.

When Dad used to take me from Swaziland and Mozambique, his car would disappear on the weekends and would come back before we needed to leave. On a total fluke, I had gone to Helena's house and saw my dad's car in the garage with all the door panels out. I didn't think much of it but I later found out it was for the smuggling of arms between the two countries. We were taking guns and live ammunition over the border between my school trips.

He laughs incredulously, then shares a particular memory, a trip back to Swaziland they made at night.

We had crossed the border and were on a long patch of gravel road. I was asleep, but woke up when Dad put the brakes on. I thought it was a broken down bus, but there was a huge rhinoceros in the road. It turned and looked at the car, and then walked away. Thank God we didn't hit it, because we would have been smithereens!

It was a "huge, huge risk" that his parents took with their son in the vehicle. "But there is no way I could criticise them. That was what they needed to do at the time."

And the fast-track growing up was thrilling for a young man. He says

I was pretty independent while I was in Swaziland. I swear, I grew up from a child to adolescence as soon as I got there. I didn't have my mum and dad there, so Swaziland opened my eyes as a teenager. I learned to smoke, I had a motorbike and could drive myself. I had older friends so that's also where I first got drunk, and had a girlfriend.

"Although there were no parents to say Don't do this or that, I also knew to push boundaries without going off the rails. I enjoyed the independence. I passed my exams and kept my feet on the ground."

And then … they moved again.

We spent a few years together as a family in Zimbabwe, straight after (that country's) independence. That was another transition. Vik and I were some of the first students of colour at Milton High School, Bulawayo, with children who had grown up in segregation under a racist government. It was the first time we experienced overt racism. But we were old enough to defend ourselves. We could confront people and deal with them – and actually, they listened and understood. Things changed. So much so that I became the first black rugby vice-captain for the second rugby team and Vik was squash captain. Then I was made a prefect, and head of house as it was a boarding school.

Zimbabwe was another operation for the movement. His parents' work intensified.

We lived in Bulawayo and people would come to the house if they were travelling to other parts of the world. I remember meeting Jacob Zuma, Cyril Ramaphosa and others. I knew how important their work was at that time, being a bit older. The house in Bulawayo became a transition hub for cadres.

Another flashback from Zimbabwe was a detention of sorts.

We were all sleeping and the house was raided by Zimbabwean armed forces. We were put into a jail, a prison camp of some kind. I just remember my mother being very upset because there were people who thought we were collaborators with apartheid state.

When, on a different occasion, I talk to Nkosinathi's brother Vikela, he fills in some of the gaps in the storyline here. "We lived next door to what they called the Green House, where many of the ANC exiles congregated. I was twelve, and at that point I began to understand that Mum was involved in the military side of the ANC," he says,

> the culmination of this when we all got arrested as a family. That was heart-wrenching and probably the first time I got involved in the context of being affected by our parents' work. The house was raided, the police came in and rounded us all up, threw us in the back of a police truck early one morning. They took us to one of those prison camps, where they separated us. Mum and Nana, and Dad and the boys. They really mistreated and mishandled Dad. We spent a day in that illustrious prison camp before they released us.

After school in Zimbabwe, Nkosinathi moved back to Dundee, followed by Vikela. Nkosinathi wanted to work in hospitality management. His girl-friend at the time, Louise, fell pregnant before he could complete his degree. "We decided unilaterally that there was no way I could support them while studying." The pair moved to London where he worked in the hospitality industry, working in middle management for the London Borough of Hammersmith and Fulham.

Then, around the 1990s, South Africa began to change.

> Mum and Dad were still in Africa. I had a feeling that I did want to go back, just to go and help with the rebuilding of the country. I left London with Louise – by then we had three kids – and we stayed with Mum and Dad in Pretoria.

Unfortunately, he struggled to find work and was forced to return to London after months of trying to establish a business.

> I was gutted because I had given up something I'd worked really hard for in London. Then I had to leave Louise and the kids with my parents, which really wasn't the ideal thing to do, especially because her family was not keen on her being all the way in Africa.

He tried once more to return to South Africa in 2017 at his mother's persuasion that the economy was improving.

> After my dad passed away, I came back to the country a couple of years ago to look after Mum. She wasn't in a good space physically and, again, I spent months trying to set up a business. But I found the processes very

slow and the red tape was overwhelming. People were easy to promise and not deliver. It really annoyed me, that South Africa had let me down in that sense. Sadly, I made the same mistake twice.

Although he laughs at this, he admits the unsettling also took a toll on this marriage. "C'est la vie, lesson learned," he says, "but the backwards and forwards may have put a strain on Louise and my relationship." They later divorced.

He says, in short, it meant that the impact on his life was indelibly linked to changes in South Africa and his parents' role in it.

> Yes, there was a lot going on. It did have an effect on me, but I haven't dealt with it, even at 54 years old, if I could put it that way. I realised that there are things I need to understand and try to remember so they make sense to me. There are questions, and answers I still need to get, to work out what the thinking was.
>
> My mental position ... is not what I would call healthy. I cope with it by not being confrontational and hiding my head in the sand. I am not outwardly emotional and any emotions I have I keep to myself and display them privately. I have high anxiety levels due to all of this but at least I am now able to quickly recognise triggers. I am dealing with that now.

****

Vikela Rankin says his sense of his relationship with his mother might be different from that of his siblings. "From a personal point of view, she rescued me by adopting me and bringing me in to the family. So she is responsible for me being who I am today," he says.

He lived with Joyce and Ken while his parents were "underground" on military operations.

> I was adopted at the age of six or seven. My biological father was Duma Nokwe, one of the Treason triallists and my mum was a lady who went by the name of Maude Manyosi – an alias; her real name was *Dudu Mate Mfusi* – she was one of the first women conscripted by the ANC.

Shortly after they arrived in Scotland, he remembers Joyce receiving copies of the first draft of her book, *A Window on Soweto*. "I recall not being very impressed as being described as an 'adopted son' when she spoke about her family in the biography. I asked her never to describe me as that ever again, and she never did."

Vikela thinks it is remarkable how sanitised their memories are, considering his parents' role in the liberation movement.

> Mum and Dad kept things pretty much sheltered from us. We lived a normal life, despite what was going on. We were at school, we sat at dinner tables together. In my case, I was on the periphery of what was

going on. Mum played an amazing role of really making sure we had a normal childhood, as much as possible. Now, we know a lot of kids who grew up in that particular period of time struggled with having normality in their lives.

There are significant moments that come up in our discussion, which he says only made sense to him as an adult.

If I think back to Dundee around 1978 or so, I remember that Mum was absolutely engrossed with her radio. She would tell us to be quiet when the radio was on and you couldn't disturb her. That's how she stayed in touch with what was going on in South Africa. She would stick to this radio, sort of like young people and social media now. There was one story that she was following … she would silence us immediately if it came up. It was the death and hanging of Solomon Mahlangu. I remember the name vividly … when he was sentenced and a number of appeals had failed. The day he was actually hung impacted Mum severely for a long period of time. She fell apart the day he was executed. Mum cried for days and days, she was so upset.

While his parents "made a considerable effort to keep things normal," as Vikela got older it became evident that there was enigmatic activity around their lifestyle. "I was about eleven or so when we moved to Mozambique. One didn't understand why they would take that leap. Mainly because we moved from a lush, plush lifestyle in Dundee to Maputo. In hindsight, I can understand it," he says. "There were also the movements into Swaziland and that, also in hindsight, was my Mum and Dad being involved in the support, transportation and the movement of all sorts of things for the ANC and MK."

In Zimbabwe, the boys knew that their parents were part of an important mission. "We lived on a farm for a while and we were often visited by ANC comrades. I remember the farm was bombed … blew up the side of the house where our bedroom was, I think," he says.

When we lived next door to the ANC safe house, there were lots of weekends when freedom songs were sung, particularly when there were weddings, as well as military drills. I was going on thirteen and my awareness of my family's involvement in politics was growing. In Zimbabwe, I had my first encounter with former president Jacob Zuma, who I remember delivering groceries to us. He would pick us up when we were walking from school and take us home on the back of a bakkie.

Vikela adds: "I never really felt the absence of Mum in any way or form, compared to Ollie's time when he was away from her in Soweto." Once the family was together in Scotland, they moved several times but were not separated from their parents again until they were adults. "It is a good reflection on them, because it meant we were able to keep our wits about us, particularly Samora and Allan, who were quite young at the time."

Vikela does recall Joyce disappearing for short periods while they stayed with their father.

> Towards the latter part of our time in Zimbabwe, Mum would be gone for a week or two, a month sometimes. Dad would only explain that she was doing "what she needed to do". That was in the late 80s or so. She would disappear for long periods of time, and in some cases Dad didn't even know where she was or how long she would be gone for. Later I could identify with the pain and strain of what he went through and, as I think about it, I remember the worry on his face.

The family's arrest and prison camp experience came later.

> That was probably the most harrowing experience of being a child of parents who were involved in the struggle. From that point on, a few things changed. Nkosinathi left for the UK. I left for my tertiary education a short while after as well.

Living with his mother again in her "tender years," as he calls it, it is time to fill in the missing pieces of her life story.

> We've not really highlighted Mum's political experiences as a family. The political side of her ... we need to think of it and dig deeper, especially because her memory isn't what it was. I know about the accolades and her role, the contribution – and I appreciate it – but, to be honest, I've never seen her as anything else, aside from Mum.

****

For Dominic Tweedie, Shanthie's husband, their sunset years are happy, although in the broader scheme of things, he sometimes feels quite despondent.

> The anti-apartheid movement as a whole had a large element of people who wanted South Africa to be exactly what is was, but non-racial ... purged of the stain of racism. As for all other things, they would remain as they were, even the inequality between rich and poor. It took us a long time to feel the extent of that. When we came back, we were in Lombardy East and had friends in Yeoville; it took me a long time to reconcile the difference between the milieu of these awfully nice people

who had no politics. They were against the National Party and racism, as they thought, but were not class-conscious.

Dominic believes that this is problematic in creating true change.

His feeling after 25 years in South Africa is that "actually, I'm afraid nothing has changed."

> I am glad we were trying to do a bit of good work, I am not sorry about that, but it hasn't changed and the struggle continues. It has been an intellectual struggle, to motivate and mobilise and rationalise the nature of the struggle in a convincing way. But other fronts ... especially the hard line that Shanthie stuck to, haven't been realised. The Kenyan author, Ngũgĩ wa Thiong'o wrote a book called *The Writer in a Neo-colonial State*, and he says: "As the struggle continues and intensifies, the lot of the writer in a neo-colonial state will become harder, and not easier." To me it translates as "The struggle that is yet to come is far harder than the struggle we have had so far."

For the younger generation, Shanthie's niece, Zoya Naidoo, says while there is a feeling of discontent in parts of South Africa's current state of affairs, the generations that followed learned humility and patience from their elders. One of their aims in the current development in South Africa is to continue the "sentiment of sacrificing their personal lives and putting themselves at risk in the struggle for liberation. They never sought any personal credit or high-profile positions."

She says the family still gather for discourse and dinner, albeit under less urgent circumstances, and for celebrations such as birthdays, anniversaries and Diwali. She feels she has been privileged to have had "forefathers and mothers who made the choices that they did, in their lives."

> Ours is a story of the perseverance of an Indian family in the long and difficult struggle for the freedom of all South Africans, and its sacrifices over many generations. It has been a 120-year struggle for freedom in South Africa ... and it isn't over, really. From satyagraha to the armed struggle, almost every member of this family has endured and experienced detention, banning, house arrest, exile and police brutality.
>
> The passion and desire to fight for a free and just society were instilled in our generation from a very young age. We all shared and continue to share a desire to stand up and fight for what is right and just.

She adds:

> Growing up in this family has definitely afforded us a very unusual but special upbringing. We had front row seats to the struggle from an early age, introducing a value system that was forged by the generations

before us. This value system was influenced by the teachings of Gandhi, Dadoo, Sisulu, Luthuli, Mandela and many others of that time.

Now a trauma counsellor with Médecins Sans Frontières (MSF) (Doctors without Borders), she says theirs was not a glamorous life.

> Growing up in a family that promoted freedom rather than the amassing of wealth, from the time of my grandfather and his siblings, we were inspired by our parents and relatives who remained a constant source of strength. We found joy in learning important lessons from them. For us, the younger generation, one of the most important lessons we acquired growing up in this family is generosity of spirit.
>
> Whether it was the Marabastad house, Rockey Street, Laudium, Lenasia or even Shanthie and Ramnie's homes in the UK, there was always an open-door policy. People from all corners of the world, all nationalities, religions and races were welcome to come in at any time to spend a night or two or just to have a hot meal followed by a good, robust political discussion, says Zoya.

This spirit created homes where ideas, thoughts and strategies came to fruition and were the basis of many defiance campaigns over the years. "For us growing up in this atmosphere provided an almost unequalled opportunity to learn and develop the tactics of the struggle first hand."

Of course, her aunts were missed at family events and in the younger generation's learning, both politically and otherwise, during their exile, which was 25 years long. She says

> My siblings, cousins and I feel robbed of the time that we could have shared with such an amazing woman. Shanthie was forced to leave this country before I was born. We only got to meet her and know her much later in our lives. We did, however, grow up knowing of her ideals and courageous battles. She had the best role model a young girl could have, and definitely inspired boys, and young people growing up in a racially segregated country.

Zoya adds that the family is endlessly proud of the contribution Shanthie made to the country's liberation. And she says, during very difficult times, the elders never abdicated their roles as parent or grandparent while maintaining their responsibilities as political activists.

> Even up until today, they are, and remain, committed and dedicated foot soldiers, more determined than ever to right the mistakes of our movement. For us, we got the opportunity to view the world from a unique perspective. My aunt and others have empowered us to continue with the family legacy. We hope we don't disappoint them. We, too, have a generation to pass it on to.

11 Latter days

2017

A few kilometres from the Pretoria cells where the women were detained in 1969 are the Union Buildings. Along with the remaining of the 22 triallists, the women gathered here in their finest to receive their national orders from the president. Nondwe chose traditional wear, Shanthie a purple sari; Joyce selected a smart black suit for the occasion, and Ma Rita wore tweeds.

They were there to receive the Order of Luthuli in Silver, which is an honour granted by the president of the time "for contributions to South Africa in the following fields: (i) the struggle for democracy, (ii) building democracy and human rights, (iii) nation-building, (iv) justice and peace, and (v) conflict resolution."[1]

The badge of the order is an equilateral triangle depicting a flintstone above a clay pot. Above the flintstone is an image of the sun, just rising, above the Isandhlwana battlefield, below the national flag. The flintstone is flanked by two animal horns rising out of the clay pot, which bears the initials AL, after Albert Luthuli, president of the African National Congress (ANC) from 1952 to 1967. Isandhlwana, the battlefield of the Anglo-Boer War, in this case, symbolises peace and tranquillity, and the leopard skin bands around the base of the horns represent Chief Luthuli's headdress. The order reads: *"Their brave fight against apartheid. They suffered but stood fiercely with the courage of their convictions for their freedom."*

The orders are displayed in the women's homes.

A tribute on the presidency website highlighted the significance of this case:

> (The arrest) was related to activities that took place a few years after the landmark Rivonia Trial. In the aftermath of the banning of the political organisations in which political activity was severely repressed, activists were driven underground or locked up in prisons. The activists constituted themselves into a powerful motor force for the regrouping of the resistance movement. Their actions inspired enthusiasm for organisation and mobilisation as well as for new forms

DOI: 10.4324/9781003228905-12

of political formation and struggles. The intention of the apartheid state was largely defeated.

The presidency noted that in 1969 the 22 people were arrested for maintaining their commitment to the ANC. "Most of these men and women had been leading members of the ANC prior to its banning, the South African Congress of the Trade Unions, the ANC Women's League and the Transvaal Indian Congress."

The women were tied together by the trial, but for the most part they all went on to live separate lives after it ended. At the ceremony in Pretoria, they spent time with each other briefly. It was the first time they had seen each other in decades. Nondwe and Shanthie met for the first time since the trial, each knowing their fate was once tied together and how both had contributed to the trial's collapse. Winnie Mandela did not attend due to ill health. She had received national orders the year before, accepted by her granddaughter Zoleka.

From afar the women had watched the goings-on in South Africa. Some friendships were maintained from a distance. By then, being separated by exile for 25 years meant that their lives grew apart and for some, ideals had changed. Shanthie says:

> Whenever we saw Winnie, she was overtly friendly. But she had her own way of doing things. I think sending her to Brandfort and the detentions, solitary confinement was the worst form of torture. We can't expect her to be the same person after that.

Joyce said simply: "Winnie was my mentor. A big sister."

While Nelson Mandela was president, he and Winnie visited Nondwe in the Eastern Cape. "After that, I didn't see her for many years. She had her life," said Nondwe.

The women would meet again shortly after the awards ceremony, this time at Winnie Mandela's funeral, in April 2018. Nondwe said: "I had to come. There was no way I was not going to be there."

****

There were many who fought, who were jailed, tortured, their lives derailed by apartheid and the fight against the regime. But this trial, the Trial of 22, was among those that changed the history of South Africa. Had the witnesses in the trial testified, Winnie Mandela and other key figures such as photographer Peter Magubane, who recorded so much of the country's history through his camera lens, would have been jailed and essentially disabled.

Perhaps the Soweto uprising of 1976, the riots and micro-revolutions, many protests and pickets, bloodshed and unshakeable organising which led the country to the brink of civil war and finally democracy might have come about in a different way.

Yet now, in their homes, these women live ordinary, quiet lives.

At another visit with Shanthie and Dominic, we share a delicious vegetarian lunch – a fresh green salad, curried potatoes and a bean stew. She shows me photographs of her grandnieces and nephews, of which there are many in the lounge, among the potted plants she coos over. The parquet floors are polished. Their days are restful. Sometimes Shanthie spends her time visiting Ramnie, who returned from exile with her family post 1994.

I can't help wondering: if someone passed this woman at the nursery, adding plants to her collection, would they guess how the defiant line she took changed the course of a country's history?

Nondwe and Ma Rita attend veterans' meetings and otherwise go about their latter days.

Ma Rita's nephew, Gadi, who lives nearby, visits for her hearty oxtail, but if he's later than 3 pm, he turns away from her gate because she rests in the afternoons. The Ahmed Kathrada Foundation prepared a booklet on her life at her recent birthday celebrations. An unassuming affair, she scolds that it was not as well attended as she expected and reminds me that there may not be too many more of these events.

Nondwe, despite her spirited nature, watches the goings-on in the political sphere earnestly. Frowning at incidents she considers bad politics, she says:

> All these young guys of the 1980s and 1990s, they don't care and they don't know. They have never been in jail, arrested or been in solitary. If they knew, they would care more about their freedom. Look at us, we are free today.

As Joyce prepares to leave our meeting, I ask her about how she feels about the state of South Africa considering her role in getting here. She takes a moment, then says:

> Democracy will always be a challenge. In South Africa, the racial divide is so deeply entrenched. On the other side, power has made some people corrupt. We never know what is in a person to make them forget their work and the discipline of the movement, to become corrupt.

"There is still a lot of work to be done, economically and more. But I always think, we must look to the good people, and there are so many who did good." We walk into a bookshop, and she spots former Intelligence minister Ronnie Kasrils' book as one she has on her reading list. She says: "It is useful to go back to the reasons we all did what we did, neh?"

I say goodbye, and she smiles warmly. Watching her walk slowly to her car, she looks like anybody's gogo (granny) in her smart beret and comfortable shoes. Few would guess where those feet had walked.

Note

1 The Presidency, n.d.

12 On healing

South African society has several decades of formalised dysfunction to recover from, and several hundred years of colonialism before then. If we consider that time frame that established our DNA and collective consciousness today, where are we in the timeline of healing?

Apartheid in South Africa was entrenched as a result of the election of the National Party government in 1948. Although "apartheid" as a concept of separatism existed prior to this, the laws and projects of that government such as the Immorality Act, which prohibited racially mixed marriages, the Group Areas Act of 1950 and the lower standards of Bantu Education, saw South Africa society divided along racial lines in all areas of life. For some of the world apartheid and its rigid policies of separation along racial lines were unfathomable; in retrospect, it is even more unfathomable. That the South African government actually thought that such a malfeasant and nonsensical concept was sustainable is hard to comprehend. Nevertheless, it did whatever it could to maintain the bubble it had built, despite the pressure from the outside world to change its stance.

The defiance campaigns by resistance movements that were spearheaded by the African National Congress (ANC), the Pan-Africanist Congress (PAC), the Transvaal Indian Congress and others saw a wave of activism in South Africa aimed at undermining and ultimately bringing down the government. Collectively, we now call this the "struggle," a single word to describe so much and such a long process.

In the 1960s, violent clashes with police against the separatist government included events such as the 21 March 1960 Sharpeville massacre, which resulted from protest action against the pass laws. Black people having to carry an identity document on their persons at all times and produce it on demand, in their own land, was a noose around the necks of the people who were born from the soil of the country. At least 70 people were killed by police for this act of defiance. The first state of emergency was declared shortly afterwards.

Simultaneously, members of political parties, particularly members of the PAC and ANC, were banned, detained, placed under house arrest and

DOI: 10.4324/9781003228905-13

arrested on charges from carrying banned material to "plotting acts of terrorism." The leadership, Nelson Mandela and others were arrested on suspicion of sabotage and as a result of the landmark Rivonia Trial of 1963/64 sentenced to life imprisonment.

The world watched these events unfold with horror, even if the government of the time did not believe so. The International Defence and Aid Fund (IDAF), which was set up in the 1950s, played an important role in bringing the harsh political realities in South Africa to international attention. Their fundraising in support of political activists and their families and the publications they produced, documenting and bearing witness to the atrocities, where they were able to, were an invaluable source of support. Political prisoners were defended by lawyers and sometimes saved from the gallows, or had their sentences reduced, and families who had lost breadwinners were given help to survive the sacrifice. The IDAF provided funding for the defence of the Treason Triallists, for the Rivonia Triallists, before doing the same for hundreds of detainees. Not only did they help detainees and their families survive from day to day, but the organisation created a mouthpiece around the details of apartheid that informed organisations like the United Nations and the Anti-Apartheid Movement.

John Collins, the founder of IDAF, commented on the arrogant nature of the government of the time, appalled that this form of government was allowed when the world was moving towards non-racialism. He revealed that:

> The South African Government spends an enormous amount of money on propaganda. Hostile world reactions to the Sharpeville shootings of 1960 and still more the consequent flight of capital, affected even the isolationist Afrikaners very deeply and over the last ten years universal efforts have been made to present South Africa favourably to the outside world. This effort and the vast sums of money expended upon it, have met with considerable success.[1]

He said, in 1970:

> ... large numbers of people, particularly British business men, politicians, journalists and others have been invited to South Africa, taken on guided tours, fed with various kinds of information and have returned to tell travellers' tales of the success of apartheid, of the happiness of the coloured people, of the stability and tranquillity of this smiling and beautiful land where white people certainly enjoy the highest standard of living in the world.

Collins was not buying it.

> The International Defence and Aid Fund is not in the above sense a propagandist organisation but in the course of its work it does acquire

a great deal of information about life in South Africa, particularly as it affects the non-European majority of the population. This information is always scrupulously checked and counter-checked. Then, if it seems appropriate, it is made public; we believe in letting the facts about South Africa and its practice of Apartheid speak for themselves.

If South Africa is so stable and peaceful it seems curious that so many (nearly all black or Coloured) people are imprisoned, banned, detained incommunicado in solitary confinement for months on end, harassed, spied upon, informed upon and, when all else fails, submitted to savage physical and mental torture. For a long time now we have been receiving increasingly horrifying stories of the activities of the police in political trials.

He wrote:

I believe it is of paramount importance that the world, and the whites in South Africa, should know clearly and in detail what methods are being used to impose the dogma of apartheid upon some 15 million allegedly grateful non-Europeans. At the present time, in Great Britain, there is widespread controversy surrounding the proposed visit of the white South African cricket team. This has produced, as a kind of side issue, discussion about the nature and practice of apartheid. To read the correspondence columns of British newspapers, to study the utterances and writings of some public figures in Britain, is to be made aware once again of the success of South African propaganda machine and of widespread ignorance about the true nature of the present policies of the white South African Government.

Collins continued:

This Government, in fact, maintains a police state of a peculiarly corrupt and vicious nature. But people have a remarkable capacity for not believing what they do not want to believe, and not seeing or hearing what they do not want to see or hear.

This capacity is very evident among white South Africans, and also unfortunately among the British people whose interest it is to do business with South Africa, to play games with white South Africa and to visit South Africa for holidays in the sun. "Bridges" such as these have existed for more than 40 years and "whites only have been happily and blindly going backwards and forwards across them."

Collins' reference to "white people" extends to all South Africans today. While few can claim to be ignorant as some in 1970, there are varying levels of the unknown among South Africans who do not know details – or do not want to know. And then those, like the corrupt, who seemingly disregard the facts despite their own involvement in securing democracy for the country, and continue to pillage without acknowledging what it took to get to a free country.

Apartheid was a brilliant system of dysfunction – allowing some to continue with the survival of their daily lives, perhaps oblivious, perhaps in fear – and others to be the protesters who were outspoken in public, or defiant in quiet ways.

There have been paramount efforts to rectify this. The Truth and Reconciliation Commission (TRC) assembled after the end of apartheid was an attempt for perpetrator and victim to give testimony and request amnesty from prosecution under the Promotion of National Unity and Reconciliation Act, No 34, of 1995. Seven years of debriefing meant that reams of information were shared and digested. The work of the TRC was accomplished through three committees: the Human Rights Violations Committee, the Amnesty Committee, and the Reparations and Rehabilitation Committee, which analysed human rights abuses that took place between 1960 and 1994.

The TRC was empowered to grant amnesty to those charged with committing atrocities during apartheid as long as two conditions were met: the crimes had to have been politically motivated and the entire and whole truth had to be told by the person seeking amnesty. No one was exempt from being charged.

From 7,112 petitioners, around 5,400 people were refused amnesty and 849 were granted amnesty. While the commission brought forth many witnesses giving testimony about the secret and immoral acts committed by the apartheid government, there was much that was not told. On 28 October 1998 the TRC presented its report, which condemned both the liberation struggle and the apartheid government for committing atrocities.

However, to what end? The process was both lauded and pronounced flawed in many respects. The possibility of restorative justice at the commission's hearings failed women in particular, according to researcher Judy Seidman, a board member of the Khulumani Support Group for those affected by apartheid. She wrote:

> How at the end of so much digging for the truth in the TRC, so many people found themselves still bleeding from open wounds. (Women had) entrenched personal memories of the ongoing violations in the name of apartheid and connected these gendered apartheid violations with the grim consequences affecting women survivors in the post-apartheid era. They explain that black women in South Africa as a group remain mired down in poverty, without resources, without economic security, with no way out.[2]

One of the most significant acts was that the TRC did not document gender-based violence against women. "It was simply subsumed under the broader heading of 'serious ill-treatment,'" Seidman wrote.

When women were interviewed by TRC statement-takers against their list of prepared questions used by the statement-takers, no questions about rape and gender-based violence were asked and if a woman spoke about being raped or experiencing gender-based violence, the statement-taker usually did not record it.[3]

Although the TRC had evidence that women were subject to more restrictions and suffered more in economic terms than men did during the apartheid years, it failed to "recognise women as actors and activists in their own right – women who fought to defend their families, defend their lives and to defend political gains."

The TRC hearing transcripts do include accounts by female activists, including Zubeida Jaffer, Barbara Hogan, Shanthie Naidoo, Winnie Mandela and others, which speak to the women's incarceration and touch on the torture of prisoners. There is no mention of mental health considerations, nor are there any detailed accounts from the women in this story, who were briefly interviewed among 20,000 others. Shanthie Naidoo, for instance, was interviewed for a few minutes in total, alongside her brothers, who gave lengthy testimonies.

Professor Malegapuru Makgoba wrote about attending the last day of the TRC.

> Cross-examination resembled more of a court proceeding than a hearing to establish the truth. Indeed, many gained the distinct impression that the lawyers were more interested in seeking evidence for future prosecutions than trying to establish the truth.
>
> At the end of the hearings I found three things missing – the truth, the lack of context in which things were occurring and the total absence of medical or forensic and psychiatric or psychological analysis of the witnesses and evidence.
>
> Cross-examination was amateurish, if not inept, at times and some legal eagles were fast behaving like robins. The contradictory evidence by witnesses made it impossible to find the truth. If the same witnesses give differing versions, there can be no truth. Even when two witnesses corroborate each other's evidence, one lacks a sense of trust. Can corroboration of evidence help in establishing the truth when the corroborators are thugs and/or pathological liars? If several witnesses describing the same incident give different versions, what then is the truth?

Makgoba wrote:

> Even the so-called eminent persons contradicted each other. At the end, one is left with the philosophical truth that there is no truth. At the best of times the truth is difficult to establish when one deals with normal trustworthy citizens. It is even harder to find when one deals with people whose values, morals and judgements are irreversibly damaged by a brutal system of oppression.[4]

Makgoba conceded that what did come out of the hearings was the brutality of the system, that families were being dismantled piecemeal and people brutalised physically and psychologically.

> The resultant pathology and uncalculated human damage that was inflicted remains one of the unspoken "holocausts" of this century. Judgement, morals, values and culture in society were being systematically eroded and clouded by the incipient and corrosive nature of the apartheid system. No-one seemed to care how brutalised and damaged the ... families were. All we wanted was to extract the truth. I find this logic difficult to understand.[5]

He added:

> For our nation to expect the truth from such traumatised individuals says something about ourselves. This is particularly so when the truth is sought without political and psychiatric contexts. There were no psychologists, psychiatrists or forensic experts to contextualise or analyse some of the witnesses' statements or personality profiles. Many witnesses were timid, nervous, with roving eyes and were uncomfortable at times.[6]

****

When reparations were first considered, economic compensation was the first tangible attempt at helping and assisting victims of apartheid and contributors to the struggle. Not for the first time in world history had this been considered an option for repairing atrocities. In the late 1980s, the US apologised to 82,000 Japanese Americans unduly imprisoned during World War 2. They were paid $20,000 to compensate for their suffering. In Germany, following the Nuremberg Trials of the Nazi Holocaust, survivors received similar payments.

The TRC attempted to compensate victims monetarily, but this proved to be both a logistical and a financial difficulty. Sadly, by 2003, only a small percentage of those who fitted the TRC categories of defined victims (the so-called KATS categories – Killings, Abductions, Torture and Severe Ill-Treatment and Bodily Harm) had given statements – let alone received compensation. More than 22,000 statements were recorded.

After accepting the TRC's final report, the state decided to give final reparations to 16,100 people and the amount paid out has been a quarter of that recommended by the TRC commissioners.

There are some 40 million South Africans who were and will continue to be affected by apartheid. If everyone were to be compensated, it would have bankrupted the fiscus which was by then already in dire need of resuscitation – not taking into consideration the current context.

The systems put in place to do reparations were also flawed. For instance, the work of the TRC Unit in the Department of Justice, where the President's Fund was also located, has not been transparent. Apartheid victims were meant to be compensated in the form of cash pay-outs after the Department of Justice and Constitutional Development gazetted into law the proposed regulations on reparations payments to apartheid victims and their children. According to those regulations, those eligible included "people who suffered physical, mental or emotional injury" during apartheid. A Sisyphean task. The department was warned that incorrectly privileging certain victim groups could lead to fresh resentment, renewed trauma and further litigation.

Former TRC commissioner and head of the commission's investigative unit Dumisa Ntsebeza SC said, in a newspaper interview in 2017, that nearly two decades after the ad hoc restorative justice body made its recommendations to provide relief for victims, the President's Fund, which was established in order to finance the recommended reparations, had grown to around R1.5 billion while thousands of victims continued to suffer.

"I'm getting close to giving up on whether the government actually appreciates the pain of those victims of apartheid atrocities who need reparations," he said.

> It's amazing that a fund that was established at the turn of the century has still not benefited those for whom it was intended. I've reached a point where I'm completely disappointed in the manner in which the President's Fund has either been financed or has dealt with whatever funds there are. I haven't had any indication that the kinds of beneficiaries who should have been recipients of the proceeds of the fund are actually getting anything.
>
> We recommended R2 000 per month for a period of six years. And we believed it would not have cost the fiscus any more than they would have been able to recover from the implementation of the wealth tax, which we also suggested.[7]

Marjorie Jobson, the national director of Khulumani, said there are well over 100,000 people with legitimate claims for reparations, and that the TRC only reached people who represented the more advantaged victims.

Many perpetrators refused to testify before the commission, or were denied amnesty, yet the government had managed to charge only a handful of perpetrators for apartheid violations. Some made public apologies; others simply took their deeds and their trauma to their death beds.

In recent years, apartheid-era death in detention inquests have been reopened and considered after perpetrators were long dead. The focus on healing in this way was a missed opportunity while rebuilding was going on in the Mandela and Mbeki years. We need not mention the decade lost to state capture and reparation. Prosecution and recouping of those years are another hurdle. Immediacy is always the current crisis.

"This is a fundamental betrayal that needs to be fixed if we're going to restore trust between citizens and political leaders," said Jobson.

> We learned that supporting people's healing without attending to their desperate needs for economic survival – why reparations and compensation are crucial to restoring the dignity and capacity of victims to take their lives forward – merely unlocked more trauma so that most survivors of atrocities still live today in states of continuing extreme stress.
>
> The gap that remains is the role of reparations in healing. This is the basis of all our efforts to have government, the Department of Justice and TRC Unit provide the ring-fenced budget for community reparations available to our organised member groups. The TRC Unit has made no progress in awarding victims this kind of support. They remain bogged down in serving only the 16 800 individuals who were fortunate to be given a number during the working life of the TRC for victims. The actuarial projection of the number of individuals who should have received this number was a minimum of 120 000 people.
>
> This is why South Africa has lost much of the acclaim it received for its TRC. Other countries have overshined South Africa by instituting a continuing victim-registration process. This has become a best practice.[8]

Jobson cites examples of countries like Côte d'Ivoire, which set up a new commission after its own TRC closed, to ensure compensation for victims. And in Colombia, six million victims of its political conflict were registered, a large proportion of whom were provided with reparations. She says this is particularly relevant in South Africa

> where the TRC followed the democratic transition so closely, at a time when major shifts were under way such as the reincorporation of homelands back into the body politic. These areas remain the places where some of the worst atrocities have never been addressed.[9]

Jobson is of the view that problems started at the very beginning. She says

> The TRC statement-taking processes were hugely flawed. The young people tasked with taking statements were told to terminate any interview in which the victim broke down emotionally while reporting what had happened to them. This meant that the stories of hundreds if not thousands of the most seriously harmed people were never captured.
>
> There has been no movement on these critical matters in South Africa despite years of engagements with the relevant departments and with Parliament. The TRC report with recommendations on reparation and rehabilitation was handed to President Mandela on 29 October

1998. That means the passing of 22 years during which time no coherent and comprehensive reparation policy has been put in place',[10] Jobson says incredulously.

The pressure to abolish apartheid was less a moral one than an attempt to quell complete anarchy and economic sanctions from the rest of the world. It is no mean feat to rebuild from the ground up with the complications of economic disparity which remained, even when the laws were erased and there was extreme strain on a system that was left. No doubt, it will take multiple years to correct.

****

There are learnings from other countries that have had to create forms of healing. The aftermath of the Northern Ireland conflict showed that storytelling can add to peace-building and repair. Research around that conflict by academic Graham Dawson shows that

> this transformation entails the imagining of "new futures", but it also requires a more complex understanding of temporality itself, to replace neat chronological categorisations that consign conflict to the past, and obscure the need for longer-term ... constructive social change over time.[11]

Storytelling brings the narrative into the present and acknowledges it. Airing it and letting it be in our present. Dawson wrote that effecting change and peace-building involves the creation of "transformative platforms, ongoing social and relational spaces" of popular participation, engagement, and mutual interchange in the public sphere.[12] In summary, simply speaking about the past can help to create a better present and future and assist in healing.

Perhaps telling and retelling the story of the Trial of 22 might have helped the women heal themselves.

There are academic studies that explicitly link solitary confinement to post-traumatic stress disorder (PTSD), a mental health condition which is triggered by a terrifying or traumatic event – either experiencing it personally or witnessing it. Symptoms may include flashbacks, nightmares and severe anxiety, as well as uncontrollable thoughts about the event – Shanthie Naidoo's continuing nightmares 50 years later, for instance. In the treatment for both victims and witnesses – in South Africa, this could mean society as a whole – it is important first to acknowledge and then release the feelings associated.

Joyce, Shanthie, Ma Rita and Nondwe all showed the early typical examples of having gone through difficulties adjusting and coping, but with time they have managed to continue their lives. Over the years, they have all experienced intrusive memories, avoidance of discussion, changes in thinking and mood and reactions that varied in waves of intensity over time, and could be triggered by reminders.

For the broader population, this can be an ongoing process. Not just for political detainees in South Africa, but for the general public, and especially for women. One of the reasons for the Khulumani group's formation was that

> many people who suffered gross human rights violations in the struggle for freedom and democracy and who sacrificed to give birth to this democracy still have not found repair or healing for the harms done to them during those times.

Jobson says Khulumani's work since its inception has been based on story-telling. "The name means 'Speak Out' so speaking has been a main thread of our work. In collective meetings of victims and survivors, people tell their stories. These happen in most areas once a month. In some areas, the meetings are more frequent,"[13] she says.

The organisation has a database built on survivors' records. It includes the stories of what happened to them, how their experiences have affected them and the needs that have arisen from the violations they experienced.

> Survivors join Khulumani by filling in a detailed needs assessment form. We have tried to train the people in the field who have assisted survivors to fill the forms in listening skills. Our very first Khulumani group at Sharpeville started the first Khulumani National Campaign called "Find Your Voice."

"Thus began our continuing efforts to support victims and survivors through creating opportunities for them to tell their stories, given that the first step in healing from serious human rights violations is for victims to be heard, acknowledged and recognised,"[14] Jobson says.

The group also facilitated a process called "Healing of Memories."

> We introduced that process to some Khulumani groups in the Eastern Cape. The stories of the extent of some of the worst atrocities in the country emerged from these workshops in former homelands. We adopted the Healing of Memories model because being organised into support groups means that social capital and trust is developed in the process, building a deeply committed group of former activists who become powerful local organising groups.[15]

Considering the economic effects, Jobson says:

> This story-telling process forms the basis of the economic empowerment processes that we introduce to these committed groups. This is based on many findings about how victims and survivors of gross

human rights violations are left behind. (Psychologist) Tony Reeler's research into the impacts of these serious violations showed the difference in all economic household measures between households that escaped any gross violations of human rights, and households in which there were at least one victim of torture and other forms of serious ill-treatment. We learned how households where one or more individuals were seriously violated, started with major setbacks. These households were more impoverished than those not affected in this way.[16]

From Guatemala, they introduced the storytelling processes as a form of healing in the mental health sphere.

> This was a model used for survivors of torture and war trauma. It identified the indigenous healers in communities in Guatemala and empowers them to provide safe spaces for storytelling. We found this a very powerful process especially for torture survivors. The first site of implementation was in Kagiso township in Krugersdorp where torture survivors had attended individual sessions of one-on-one psychotherapy. The review of this work revealed to us that our community-based processes were more effective than individual psychotherapy,[17] Jobson says.

Other offshoots of the trauma, according to Khulumani, may contribute to the high levels of domestic violence reported in early assessments.

> This is where South Africa became the world leaders in gender-based violence with present statistics bearing evidence of the failure of the state to understand what serious human rights violations result in over time. As the silence about rape emerged as a result of the one billion rising campaign, we introduced extensive work on addressing gender-based violence. A Khulumani Men's Forum was established.[18]

Khulumani then became involved in developing its own process of Art and Narrative for Healing and Heritage, which has been implemented at scattered sites across the country.

> The programme in community-based psychosocial rehabilitation uses visual arts and community narrative processes to create spaces where group members explore their experiences and their understanding of the events through which they lived. For thousands of survivors of the abuses and atrocities of South Africa's past, there have been no opportunities to deal with the trauma they experienced as activists in the struggle against apartheid. The participatory art and narrative process creates a way for survivors of these atrocities to deal with the trauma associated with the violations they endured to reclaim their dignity, mourn their losses and begin to assert their agency,[19] she says.

All of the endeavours allow people to recognise their individual capacities.

> Combined with the possibilities of working as a member of a collective, they become increasingly self-reliant as participants in actively shaping their own futures and histories. This is a critical process of becoming able to *"make something of their citizenship"*, as we call it, and to fulfil expectations of making contributions to the well-being of their families and communities.
>
> We had to then understand what was key to keeping our groups functioning and meeting regularly. We worked with Dr Sandra Bloom, a psychiatrist who created a process that is critical for institutional culture change. We took this forward and became licensed to use the programme developed by Dr Bloom, called Self. It provides a framework for a group to talk through the stages of recovery from major trauma – establishing safety, learning to manage the emotions that are a normal response to major trauma, dealing with loss – a huge need because people in the struggle were not given time to mourn.

Jobson says: "The TRC was in fact a site of mourning but only 2 000 people had the benefit of the hearings process."[20]

The final step is

> taking back one's agency to start planning a future. This is the programme we are still using today with the growing demand for healing workshops. A colleague from Madrid, Spain, David Ramos Collada, who had been working in mental health issues in Colombia and Mexico and who had exposure to the social psychology of (Latin American psychologist) Martin Baro, adapted the Self model for use in Khulumani for our group-based processes. We shared this in townships across Gauteng.[21]

Jobson says while there have been some inroads, the work may never be done. The impacts, particularly economically, will be long-lasting in South Africa. It is a generational cycle that may only be broken in another 50 years.

****

The lack of ongoing personal attempts at psychological healing has no doubt had an effect on the women in this story – and on the generation that followed them. Joyce's children, who were left in South Africa during her detention and early exile, Nondwe's daughters and Ma Rita's children and grandchildren have all been affected by their mothers' absence.

There is some academic record of women who do not appear in historical texts; some were ordinary citizens whose names are not well known. Prison stories are limited and often repetitive, without individual detail.

Professor Kalpana Hiralal wrote in her study of the female narrative:

> For many women political activists their prison experiences were an important chapter in their lives in the fight against the apartheid regime. The nature of women's incarceration, interrogation, and the impact on their personal lives highlights not only the gendered aspects of imprisonment but also the heterogeneity of women's experiences.[22]

To what extent this impacted the women is hard to tell, as is the long-term physical impact. And these are only four of countless women. There are those who didn't survive; others who survived with wounds both visible and invisible. They show up in our country every single day.

When we think of the corrupt leaders whose moral compass might have been swayed by growing dejected over the long period of time, impatience for change possibly, perhaps some of this comes from those wounds. Perhaps this is on the back of those who carry the emotional burden in their places of work, triggered by racially tense moments in society – in road rage and shopping queues. Perhaps our healing is based on a weighting of who did more, who sacrificed more, who benefited more, who can remember more. What is clear is that South Africans as a nation do carry this in our collective DNA and it is in our awareness in present-day South Africa.

Professor Pumla Gobodo-Madikizela's research following her years of work documenting the TRC focuses on two areas of "moving forward," if we can refer to "looking backward" in this way. An award-winning author and editor and Professor and Research Chair for Historical Trauma and Transformation at Stellenbosch University, Gobodo-Madikizela's research explores the ways in which the impact of such "dehumanising experiences of oppression and violent abuse, continue to play out in the next generation in the aftermath of historical trauma." The second research area expands her work on forgiveness and remorse, and probes the role of empathy more deeply.

She says the TRC was a unique historical moment.

> It showed us human destruction and cruelty against other human beings, but also the capacity for empathic bonding between victims or survivors and perpetrators. I am referring to family members of victims who expressed forgiveness for perpetrators. I was intrigued by these gestures of forgiveness: what does forgiving a person who has murdered your loved ones mean? I was not aware of any precedents of this kind of response.

Although it was flawed, she says:

> There was something profoundly hopeful about the TRC. Here we were, having emerged from the darkest period of our history, engaging in a process that tried to transcend the eclipses of humanity in order to

embrace new horizons of possibility. In a way, the choice to pursue a TRC process, with all its troubling imperfections, was a sign of lessons learnt from history.

She said it was an important starting point.

The aim was to foster accountability for the past, and to restore hope and a sense of agency among people whose sense of identity was diminished and humiliated by the traumatic, social and economic legacies of apartheid. The TRC was an extraordinary opportunity for scholars interested in understanding the experience of trauma and its repercussions.

But, she says, what struck her about the most about the TRC process is how it was unusual compared to studies of mass traumatic events like the Holocaust and dealing with its aftermath through the Nuremberg Trials. "In this sense then, my research interest – on remorse and forgiveness in the aftermath of historical trauma – was an exciting new frontier in the field of psychology."[23]

Gobodo-Madikizela's extensive work, including the recent *Memory, Narrative and Forgiveness: Perspectives on the Unfinished Journeys of the Past*, brought a number of scholars together to explore the relationship between trauma and memory, and the complex, interconnected issues of trauma and narrative – storytelling – in testimonial and literary form. Most importantly, for the purposes of South Africa moving on today and in the future, it examines transgenerational trauma. The research looks into using memory as the basis for dialogue and reconciliation in divided societies, and the changing role of memory in the aftermath of mass trauma, as well as mourning and the potential of forgiveness to heal the enduring effects of mass trauma.

Multiple years of research and case study, she says, shows that under certain conditions, forgiveness in the context of dealing with past human rights violations is possible. She looked at the dynamics of historical trauma and its transgenerational repercussions – which I believe are in full effect in South Africa – and how narratives, storytelling and empathy impact this.

The women in this story have reacted positively – without hatred in their hearts. It seems illogical, but anti-apartheid organisations somehow largely succeeded in disseminating the peaceful acceptance of strife, struggle, loss of life, and the torture and mental warfare that was meted out to and in some cases, by, its soldiers. For the most part, it was noble, aligned with the nature of those who chose to get involved in it. Those who strayed off the path of the strict organisation which didn't allow infighting or disagreements to be aired publicly because it showed weakness were excluded and disciplined. After liberation, though, it got messy.

Gobodo-Madikizela says:

> The descendants now face the double jeopardy of the transgenerational repercussions of apartheid's corruption, and the failures of some politicians in our contemporary government in their moral duty to act in ways that would reduce the suffering of the descendants of those who were oppressed under apartheid.

What are the answers? She says the first non-answer is revenge, bitterness and even vengeful acts like corruption.

> In much of the world's great literature, and much of its past and current history as well, the idea of vengeance has carried with it a certain noble air, as if motivated by a force of good that somehow enables it to transcend the very violence that gave birth to it. Violent acts designed to make the other person suffer pain, are sometimes thinly cloaked under notions of "justice-seeking", "defending" human rights, or righteous indignation.
>
> They (vengeful acts) have an attraction, a logic that has come to hold a central position in the thinking and values held by individuals and groups who have been on the receiving end of the humiliation produced by oppression.

Tragically, Gobodo-Madikizela says, for some the desire for revenge is sometimes the only way a person who has experienced oppression and violence can restore their sense of dignity. "The tragic outcome of this kind of response is that it transforms victims into perpetrators, and often breeds never-ending cycles of violence," she adds.

While she says opportunities for thoughtful dialogue help build a form of "social solidarity and establish a foundation for a shared ethics of care among people who have had a time such as this," this does not apply in countries in the throes of ongoing violence. Violence in the case of South Africa right now may be not only physical, but psychological and economic. The #feesmustfall protests which saw university students shut down academic work in 2018/19 due to economic disparity is an example of both a physical and an economic protest.

Without doubt, she says there should be a parallel equalising of economic disparity along with psychological healing.

Gobodo-Madikizela's recent work *Breaking Intergenerational Cycles of Repetition: A Global Dialogue on Historical Trauma and Memory* is a study in how memory can be used as a basis for dialogue and transformation:

> I think we are engaging with these issues at a pivotal moment in South Africa where questions about the past – and how to interrupt the cycles of its repetition and bring about social change – have come to dominate public debate.

The first psychological step is in acknowledgement. "This is so crucial to survivors of traumatic experiences. Public processes of accountability, such as when perpetrators confess to massive human rights crimes are an important form of recognition that helps survivors feel a sense of affirmation and validation," she says. "One of the tragic consequences of trauma is a loss of victims' sense of agency."[24]

Unfortunately for many detainees and stalwarts who were exiled, this is not a plausible option 20 years later. For the generations after them, though, those with whom we engage every day, it is for each of us to try to identify with the other's history.

> This is an issue of concern particularly when one considers the consequences of what I call "everyday" traumas that affect communities at the margins of society. Some of the most destructive acts of violence to the human soul are the subtle, systematic acts of structural violence that undermine the dignity and sense of worth of individuals, the insidious acts of violence that result from ongoing depravity, humiliation and degradation – rather than from spectacular and extraordinary violence. The loss of a sense of agency is the most disempowering force that confronts victims because of this kind of "insidious trauma," she says.

These everyday traumas can similarly be found in the micro-aggressions that plague middle-class South Africans today. K-word trauma, road rage that turns racial, boardroom politics are some examples.

This, Gobodo-Madikizela says, is because the narrative around South Africa's history incorrectly centred on forgiveness – implying forgetting and moving on when we were not ready:

> I think that the word forgiveness is misunderstood. Some people see it as a kind of magic wand, a panacea for all the complex problems of our post-apartheid society. In my recent work, I have argued that forgiveness is the wrong word. Forgiveness seems to suggest a fixed position, or a coming to an end – "I offer you forgiveness so that I can have closure and move on." A subtext here seems to signify an act of leaving something behind, moving on without looking back.

Remorse, on the other hand, is a reclaiming of the conscience. "What happens then, is not forgiveness, but certain subtle moments, words you use, concern you show and taking responsibility, that opens up something in the victim – that you recognise they are feeling pain."

For those who say people should "move on," that we shouldn't focus so much on memory but on forgetting, she says:

> As if one had a choice in the matter when it comes to trauma? I think that ultimately, what is crucial for countries that have to face the

complicated legacies of a violent past is to try to create conditions that can foster not so much forgiveness, but rather empathy. Empathy can be a resource for expanding the vision of a shared future, a vision that takes us to the edge of emotional possibility, pointing us to a general horizon of an ethics of care. I think that if relationships were inspired by a sense of care that extends to those who are different, problems such as racism would be reduced dramatically.

Gobodo-Madizela says her feeling of where South Africa is in this process is still "deeply wounded; painfully divided."

The trauma from apartheid, which we still hold in our bodies and carry into our relationships, bleeds into different forms of violence. Some trauma is internalised as depression, loss of dignity and self-worth. There is a lot of repairing still to be done.

To begin is to know the stories and to share them, digest and understand them. From that place of learning, so much more can develop in this healing process.

Emilia Potenza, curator of the Apartheid Museum, facilitated the recent exhibition of the Naidoo family story at the museum, called "Resistance in their Blood." "When we tell the history of apartheid, we often talk in abstract terms," she said.

The discovery of gold and how that drove the demand for cheap labour. Colonialism and how it served a global system of dispossession. Large-scale agriculture that required plantation labour. Industrialisation, urbanisation, economic forces. And we talk also of the resistance to apartheid, how it was organised, which sectors of society were mobilised, which events had the most impact on the way in which the society developed.

And it is right to analyse in this way, right to look back over large swathes of time and try to understand what happened. But that kind of analysis does not tell us much about what it was like to live under apartheid. It does not tell us about the agonising choices that people had to make. About the day-to-day suffering, the day-to-day triumphs, the way in which the lives of individuals and families were shaped by the larger events under which they lived. And how they in turned shaped the events around them.[25]

Detailed stories are missing from the country's collective consciousness, let alone the history books. "Stories like these begins to correct that," she said at the opening of the exhibition. "It tells the story of one family. An extraordinary family, and yet an ordinary one. A group of people whose lives intersected with the great forces of colonialism, apartheid and the resistance movement, and how they responded."[26]

She says a key aspect to the story was their choice to be involved. 'So many people lived through the circumstances that confronted this family.

Every person, every dinner table faced the circumstances that they did. Very few responded in the way that this family did.

> It is mostly not about great men or great women but about the foot soldiers of resistance whose ongoing acts of service to a greater good propelled the struggle against racism and apartheid in South Africa over more than a century. Everyone who lived through apartheid had to make choices. Most people were simply swept along by the forces around them. Not this family. They were unusual in that they engaged in a kind of multi-generational activism. They took on the system with their bare hands. They fought at every turn. They suffered every imaginable consequence – humiliation, detention, torture, long periods of imprisonment and exile. But they did not lose their centre.[27]

This is why stories can open our minds and consciousness, in the path to healing.

Notes

1 IDAF archive.
2 Seidman, 2011.
3 Seidman, 2011.
4 Makgoba, 2018.
5 Makgoba, 2018.
6 Makgoba, 2018.
7 Ntsebeza, 2017.
8 Jobson, 2020.
9 Jobson, 2020.
10 Jobson, 2020.
11 Dawson, 2017.
12 Dawson, 2017.
13 Jobson, 2020.
14 Jobson, 2020.
15 Jobson, 2020.
16 Jobson, 2020.
17 Jobson, 2020.
18 Jobson, 2020.
19 Jobson, 2020.
20 Jobson, 2020.
21 Jobson, 2020.
22 Hiralal, 2015.
23 Gobodo-Madikizela, 2020.
24 Gobodo-Madikizela, 2020.
25 Potenza, 2016.
26 Potenza, 2016.
27 Potenza, 2016.

Conclusion

I am a generation, two, after the women in this book. They are the same age as my grandmother. Growing up as a scholar, student and news journalist, I did not know this story. Through lack of storytelling, particularly about women, we are forced to put pieces of the puzzle together without really having a 360-degree world view.

In healing, we cannot rewrite the past, or change it in any way. At the same time, we cannot forget. Once we forget, it is gone. We have to remember people like the women in this book as a foundation from which we walk through life. They can guide us when we keep them in our mind's eye as we navigate the tough, tough democracy that has shown so many fault-lines in recent years. How to do this is to know the history of our forefathers, and particularly the period 1942–92. Fifty years that did not stand still in South Africa. They moved in lives, love and relationships.

The stories of Joyce's love story, Ma Rita's tragedy, Nondwe's quiet, unwavering loyalty. Their values are in the wise words of the poet Rabindranath Tagore who influenced Shanthie's forefathers: "Man's abiding happiness is not in getting anything but in giving himself up to ideas which are larger than his individual life, the idea of his country, of humanity, of God."

The children and grandchildren of the hundreds of thousands of stalwarts are among our peers today. Reviving such stories from the past can change the way we think and carry ourselves in our interaction with them, and if we recognise that we are one of them ourselves through our common DNA.

These are stories that should inspire our sons and definitely our daughters, my daughters. When we read of rebel girls and brave girls, the quiet voices are often the ones that made the most difference. The loud voices always stand out, but we must hear from the unspoken too.

It may not have been in everyone's capacity or ability to contribute and make change, but for those who chose to do it, we can still look up and be grateful. Without feeling like we ourselves did not contribute, acknowledgement and appreciation of what they did for little reward, and great retribution, is eternal. For my daughters and theirs, we can draw strength from those who came before us.

DOI: 10.4324/9781003228905-14

Why the women? Because throughout time, the stories of women are different to the stories of men. It may continue to be this way for years ahead – until we change it.

The focus on these particular women – Joyce, Shanthie, Ma Rita and Nondwe – is to record their story from their unique perspectives while considering the long-term effects. While the tribulations of Robben Island were atrocious, there was some marked differences, perhaps because it was closely observed by the international community. In some senses, imprisonment on Robben Island was communal. There was reading material, soccer games, chess matches along with the back-breaking physical labour – something to do. People studied via correspondence, wrote letters and prepared manuscripts for their release.

Without diminishing the inhumane circumstances and the usually very lengthy periods of incarceration, the other cog in the machinery, venues of detention and torture around the country, were *differently* awful. Johannesburg's John Vorster Square, named after the justice minister who introduced torture to the apartheid laws, is rife with ghosts of heroes such as Neil Aggett and Ahmed Timol – and there are many more.

The Old Fort at Constitutional Hill and Pretoria Central where women were kept are stark, dark and damp. In solitary confinement, some were kept naked, others not allowed to wash, most not allowed out even for exercise. Most were denied sanitary material. Food was devoid of nutrition; when it came, sandy, rancid and rotten were the options. Narrow cells with high, thick walls, either blindingly dark or so brightly lit by the single electric light bulb would drive a person insane.

More than 100 detainees died.

This story started with Winnie Mandela's death and the prison visit on that chilly day in April 2018, the anniversary of the hanging of Solomon Mahlangu. I imagined how Winnie must have felt, in the dark, cold space. The suicidal thoughts, the lack of medical treatment, days of sleep deprivation that might have contributed to her eventual demise from kidney failure. And all the while in prison, how she would have blocked thoughts about her children from her mind. The thought of two young girls like my own, almost starving in their parents' absence, was heart-breaking. Her banishment to Brandfort, in the ironically named Free State, away from her support structure and social circle must have tormented her. Labelled a terrorist, her neighbours were either afraid of her or scornful of the dangerous woman locked away in her meagre house.

Yet, she rose and grew into a world-renowned figure of liberation, albeit side-lined at times by the organisation she served so passionately. And then, in death, her very human behaviour was remembered unkindly and with bias.

My thoughts went to how her prison experience must have contributed to her emotional state thereafter, her every action in life determined by the role she had to play while the leaders were kept away. They may have been imprisoned, but she was on the frontlines of the decades' long battle.

Questions about her life – and detention – were left unanswered. What impact did it have on her as a woman and as a mother, as a politician who was tasked with leading the resistance movement on the ground? Organising the banned African National Congress (ANC) comrades and cadres, pushing the country slowly towards democracy after the movement would first bring the country to boiling point, burning and bleeding.

Her role as a nation builder was recognised, but eulogies were delivered in a tarnished, diminished urn by international and local media. The *Sydney Morning Herald* called her "mother, then mugger, of new South Africa." *The Economist* called her a "dangerous woman." "Nelson Mandela's wife" was how she was mentioned by several publications. A *City Press* editorial referred to the anticipated arrival of Nelson Mandela from prison in 1990, and how Winnie left their Soweto home at 2 am, with her "lover at the time, Dali Mpofu." Photographs of her in military regalia accompanied obituaries.

It was as if there was a collective, separate mourning for the woman who, in 1969, was grabbed by police while her two young daughters tugged at her skirt, crying. At the time her husband, the leader of the movement, was in prison. Millions of people looked to her for guidance. She faced daily harassment for her unrelenting defiance of those in charge. Unable to move or socialise freely as a banned person, the security branch turned her friends into spies, made her paranoid about those around her and followed this up with detention, isolation and torture.

It is one of the reasons the story of this unique trial went unknown and unrecognised in the last five decades. We don't go there. And for the minority who *do* remember, it was at best obscure, at worst distorted.

This is a *her*story, still alive and evolving at the time of writing in 2019. It makes us uncomfortable to hear these stories, but we risk worse if we don't – apathy, and a skewed moral compass, which many already follow. We have seen how leaders and those involved in the struggle went rogue. Of course there were reasons, many reasons. Perhaps being forgetful about the road to where we are today is one of them.

Dealing with our collective consciousness was neglected in the process of rebuilding the country post liberation. When the stories of these women are published, I hope it will encourage others to pursue their past and experiences on a psychological level to ultimately help heal and build a better society – wherever they are in the world.

****

Storytelling in the form of journalism is indelibly linked to narratives from that time, when material was banned and as little as possible was recorded to prevent it getting into the wrong hands. There is a strong thread around sharing information in this story. Their formal and informal means of communication – the meetings, the pamphlet distribution, the apartheid-era newspapers in South Africa and in the supportive countries outside its borders – without sophisticated technology shows how the written word was so valued and so threatening that many people were thrown in jail for scraps of paper found in their homes. The detention was largely for these activists to be silenced.

The accounts of journalism in this story were almost nostalgic, in the context of the disrepair that the current-day media now experiences. Despite social media and technology delivering stories to wider audiences at every millisecond, how much goes missing in the noise is a pity.

Today we have different issues that are creating silence around stories – attention, care, compounded by industry woes. We have evolved to the other end of the spectrum of knowledge and learning from the 1969 story – too much shared, with much of it of little value, not sure what is truth. But building intellectual capital, almost a form of meditation on valuable information, seems to be on the rise. It should not be a privilege to learn, think and reflect on these stories, especially if we are to embrace them and carry them with us, in a light manner that doesn't weigh us down but as useful, functional knowledge.

South Africa's history is recent. The most significant war was largely fought in the mind – it was a psychological, classist and racial war. The detail is therefore valuable. To know about the positive, hopeful stories is also important, not only for the bravery and courage shown, but for the love and friendship that can be found in the lives and the daily existence of South Africans while the wheels of history turned. In reflecting on my own career of the last 17 years, I've often felt that I missed an important era of journalism. Apartheid-era journalists were part of the recording, organising and putting bricks in place; and the generation that came after recorded the build-up to democracy and the birth of the rainbow nation. My era – not exclusively but largely – covered the aftermath: corruption, celebrity and conspicuous consumption. Social media arrived. While it influenced #metoo and #amInext, it also diluted stories, changed narratives and shaped a post-truth world of information that both expands and confuddles the mind.

The simultaneous erosion of the media is happening alongside threads of excellence which shine through the grey sludge of everything else. It is a global phenomenon. We are in an information age, but we seem to know more than ever and less than ever.

There is also a shift towards knowledge. For all those who were blinkered or sheltered by defunct history syllabi, answers are slowly emerging, if you look. There are many, like me, who sometimes need a reminder of our unique and beautiful history while existing in the present. To put a spotlight on the emotional impact of apartheid is to humanise it further than the single narratives of iconic figures like Nelson Mandela. These stories must go beyond the Mandela effect and the parallel dark mysteries of Winnie Mandela.

****

What a privilege and education it has been to spend time with these women in my own learning. In the short space of time, April 2018 to 2020, they have aged, shrinking physically and mentally. The interviews started off as formulaic recollections of the sort they have been sharing when asked every so often in the last five decades. Then slowly, the deeper detail emerged and their lives unfolded. I have to say, the stories are not entirely complete. It would be impossible to capture everything, and what they consider important and not, which shows their humanity and tells a life story.

Like the elders who have left the world, the stories of the "younger radicals" will go with them. But for a while, they are here and we can spend time in their presence. It is immeasurably gratifying that they have allowed me to revisit parts of their 50 years of history, to spend precious time with them, sharing pain but also laughter and lucid memories, side stories which were not for print. And to get to know them, just a little.

Pulling together the significant moments and putting together their pieces of the puzzle that makes up the timeline of a rich history has been a privilege that I do not take lightly.

Their children and grandchildren are our peers and contemporaries. When we think of them, we must remember that through collective DNA, ours and theirs are the same, strand for strand. As South Africans, women, free thinkers, we will always find connectivity.

The focus on mental wellbeing is at the forefront of our conversation as could be the greatest scourge on our health as a global community. For those of us who battle – with post-partum depression, the "baby blues," the daily assault of pull-her-down syndrome, the mental load from running our complex lives, homes, careers; and those who were traumatised by regimes like the apartheid regime, or femicide and gender-based disparity and violence. These remain women's challenges until we unravel and address them. The struggles may be different to the women in this story, but they are struggles none the less.

As I continue my own life, knowing there are two young girls who I must guide and mould, I can only show by example how empathy and the understanding of another's journey can lead us to behave and act differently, with conviction.

It may be a small contribution in documenting this long journey which had many actors and many directors, side acts and secondary stories, but it was longing to be told.

The children who were affected especially, particularly Nkosinathi "Ollie" Rankin, shared thoughts and memories that they had never delved into before. The value is immense, as the case studies reflect. If school history texts shaped events in time around storytelling of human lives, rather than dates of wars and treaties, perhaps the value would be visible already. Too many stories, women's stories, go unheard. I know that Joyce was in the process of telling her story several decades later when her memory started to fade. Her children, born across continents, each have different pieces of her story in them which they have still not fully shared with her or each other, let alone outsiders.

These were special human beings, as were those who supported them. We can take inspiration from the grandmothers – Amelia, Nellie, Ama – who encouraged these young women to go out and do their work, knowing at what risk their children did this.

In the time of the completion of my studies at Wits university which resulted in the Master's thesis (in April 2018, inspired by Winnie Mandela's death), which in turn sparked the writing of this book, I had to remind myself that the time dedicated away from my own family was inconsequential in comparison to theirs. I took the support the women received as fuel for my own work.

For some young people, like Laurette Ndzanga, these stories may be wearying, knowing her grandmother's past. But in her own journey, she keeps their story in her footsteps as she walks through present-day South Africa. As Nondwe's daughter Phila says, they might not have chosen their mothers' sacrifice, but it was for them individually as much as it was for the greater good.

These women – the everyday, ordinary, quiet foot soldiers – are our north stars, the way-finders in whichever war we face today and those yet to come. They taught us to stand on the side of the good, that we are a force on our own, but that together we have immeasurable strength.

References and source material

Author's note

Much of the material used and quoted in this book is comprised of personal interviews conducted by the author with Joyce Sikhakhane-Rankin, Shanthie Naidoo, Rita Ndzanga, Nondwe Mankahla and various members of their families over a period of time.

Ahmed Kathrada Foundation Archive. 2016. Available at: https://www.kathradafoundation.org/ and https://www.kathradafoundation.org/download/rita-ndzanga-booket/

CBS News. 2018. 'Winnie Mandela, ex-wife of Nelson Mandela, and Apartheid activist, dies at 81 after "long illness"'. Available at: https://www.cbsnews.com/news/winnie-mandela-nelson-mandela-ex-wife- apartheid-activist-dies-at-81 (Accessed April 2018).

Collins, F. 2017. 'R1.5 billion for apartheid victims but thousands still waiting for money'. Timeslive. Available at: https://www.timeslive.co.za/politics/2017-08-28-r15-billion-for-apartheid-victims-but-thousands-still-waiting-for-money/

Constitution Hill precinct. Exhibition notes.

Dawson, G. 2017. 'The meaning of 'moving on': From trauma to the history and memory of emotions in 'post-conflict' Northern Ireland'. In *Irish University Review*, 47(1): 82–102.

Dhlamini, M. 2006. Speech given at Women's Day event in celebration of the 1956 Women's March.

Dorell, O. 2018. 'Winnie Mandela, controversial ex-wife of Nelson Mandela, dies at 81'. Available at: https://www.usatoday.com/story/news/world/2018/04/02/winnie-mandela- wife-nelson-mandela-dies/477898002 (Accessed 18 April 2018).

Du Plooy, E. 2018. 'Why talking about the TRC is still important 20 years later'. Available at: https://www.news24.com/Columnists/EleanorduPlooy/why- talking-about-the-trc-is-still-important-20-years-later-20180724

East Coast Radio. 2018. 'Nelson Mandela's ex-wife Winnie Mandela dies at 81'. Available at: https://www.ecr.co.za/news/news/nelson-mandelas-ex-wife- winnie-mandela-dies-at-81/ (Accessed April 2018).

Findlay, K. 2018. 'Rewriting history: Twitter's reinvention of Winnie Madikizela-Mandela's legacy'. Available at: https://themediaonline.co.za/2018/04/rewriting-history-twitters-reinvention- of-winnie-madikizela-mandelas-legacy/ (Accessed 24 April 2018).

Gobodo-Madizela, P. The Greatest Gift to Give https://www.nihss.ac.za/sites/default/files/Newspapers/%Prof20Pumla%20Goboda-Madikizela.pdf

Hagan, B.O., Wang, E.A., Aminawung, J.A., Albizu-Garcia, C.E., Zaller, N., Nyamu, S., Shavit, S., Deluca, J. & Fox, A.D. 2018. 'History of solitary confinement is associated with post-traumatic stress disorder symptoms among individuals recently released from prison'. In *Journal of Urban Health*, 95(2): 141–8.

Hassim, S. 2018. 'Winnie Madikizela-Mandela: Revolutionary who kept the spirit of resistance alive'. Available at: http://theconversation.com/winnie-madikizela-mandela-revolutionary-who-kept-the-spirit-of-resistance-alive-94300 (Accessed 18 September 2018).

Hiralal, K. 2014. 'Married to the Struggle: For better or worse: Wives of Indian anti-Apartheid activists in Natal: The untold narratives'. In *New Contree Special Edition*, 70: 83–106.

Hiralal, K. 2015. 'Narratives and testimonies of women detainees in the anti-Apartheid struggle'. In *Agenda*, 29(4): 34–44.

Hogan, B. 2020. Testimony at the inquest into the death of Neil Aggett. Available at: https://www.news24.com/news24/southafrica/news/neil-aggett-inquest-barbara-hogan-tells-court-how-she-wishes-she-had-never-written-close-comrades-report-20200129

Isaack, W. (n.d.). 'Truth and memory: From victims to active citizens'. Khulumani Support Group. Available at: Khulumani.net (Accessed December 2018).

Jobson, M. 2020. Khulumani Support Group. Personal interview with author.

Kallan, R.A. 1975. 'Entrance', in *The Journal of Popular Culture*, 9(1): 106–13.

Khulumani Support Group. khulumani.net.

Lamche, P. 2018. *Winnie*. Video documentary. Christoph Jörg/Pumpernickel Films.

Makgoba, M. 2018. 'TRC Hearing Failed to Find The Truth'. Available at: https://www.news24.com/Columnists/GuestColumn/trc-hearing-failed-to-find-the-truth-20180415-3

Makhanya, M. 2018. 'We must not want to be Winnie'. Available at: https://city-press.news24.com/News/mondli-makhanya-we-must-not-want-to-be-winnie-20180409 (Accessed 10 April 2018).

Mathope, G. 2018. 'Winnie's post-traumatic stress disorder was never treated'. *The Citizen*. Available at: https://citizen.co.za/news/south-africa/1876444/charlene-smith-winnie-madikizela-mandelas-post-traumatic-stress-disorder-was-never-treated/ (Accessed 3 April 2018).

Mayo Clinic. 2018. 'Post-traumatic stress disorder (PTSD) – Symptoms and causes'. Available at: https://www.mayoclinic.org/diseases-conditions/post-traumatic-stress-disorder/symptoms-causes/syc-20355967 (Accessed June 2018).

Mbeki, T. 2006. Address at Women's Day event celebrating 50th anniversary of the 1956 Women's March.

Mhlauli, M.B., Salani, E. & Mokotedi, R. 2015. 'Understanding Apartheid in South Africa through the racial contract'. In *International Journal of Asian Social Science*, 5(4): 203–19.

Msimang, S. 2018. 'Winnie Mandela's legacy: A renewed militancy in South Africa'. In *The Washington Post*. Available at: https://www.washingtonpost.com/news/global-opinions/wp/2018/04/04/winnie-mandelas-legacy-a-renewed-militancy-in-south-africa/?noredirect=on&utm_term=.e9be348a9b0a (Accessed 18 September 2018).

Munusamy, R. 2018. 'Winnie Madikizela-Mandela's complex life of defiance'. Available at: http://www.businesslive.co.za/rdm/politics/2018-04-04-ranjeni-munusamy-winnie-madikizela-mandelas-complex-life-of-defiance/ (Accessed April 2018).

Ngoyi, L. From Sisulu, E. 2003. *Walter and Albertina Sisulu: In our lifetime.* Cape Town: New Africa Books.

Ntsebeza, D. 2017. In Collins, F. 2017. 'R1.5 billion for apartheid victims but thousands still waiting for money'. Timeslive. Available at: https://www.timeslives.co.za/politics/2017-08028-r15-billion-for-apartheid-victims-but-thousands-still-waiting-for-money

O'Malley, P. (n.d.). 'O'Malley: The heart of hope'. Available at: https://omalley.nelsonmandela.org/omalley/index.php/site/q/03lv00000.ht m (Accessed May 2018).

Omar, Z. 2016. 'The greatest gift to give . . . Reflecting on forgiveness and healing'. https://www.nihss.ac.za/sites/default/files/Newspapers/Prof%20Pumla%20Gobodo-Madikizela.pdf

Potenza, E. 2020. Speech at opening of 'Resistance in Their Blood' exhibition at the Apartheid Museum, 5 March 2020.

Rosenthal, G. 2003. 'The healing effects of storytelling: On the conditions of curative storytelling in the context of research and counselling'. In *Qualitative Inquiry*, 9(6): 915–33.

Seidman, J.A. 2011. 'How the TRC failed women in South Africa'. Khulumani Support Group. Available at: https://khulumani.net/truth-a-memory/how-the-trc-failed-women-in-south- africa-a-failure-that-has-proved-fertile-ground-for-the-gender-violence- women-in-south-africa-face-today/2011/10/03/ (Accessed May 2018).

Sikhakane, M. 2018. 'Soweto in exile: The publication history of Joyce Sikhakane's *A Window on Soweto*. PhD dissertation.

South African History Online. 2018. 'Winnie Madikizela-Mandela'. Available at: https://www.sahistory.org.za/people/winnie-madikizela-mandela (Accessed December 2018).

The Presidency. (n.d.). 'The 22 ANC Political Triallists of 1969'. Available at: http://www.thepresidency.gov.za/national-orders/recipient/22-anc-political-   triallists-1969 (Accessed April 2018).

Treatment Action Campaign. 2010. 'A tribute to comrade Barbara Hogan'. Available at: https://tac.org.za/news/a-tribute-to-comrade-barbara-hogan/

Truth and Reconciliation Commission. 1997. Human rights violations: Women's hearing. Available at: http://www.justice.gov.za/trc/special/women/ranken.htm.

Truth Commission: Special Report. (n.d.). Transcript Episode 58. Available at: http://sabctrc.saha.org.za/tvseries/episode58/section2/transcript7.htm?tab=v ictims (Accessed June 2018).

Van der Merwe, E.J., Venter, C.A. & Temane, Q.M. 2009. 'Untold stories of a group of black South Africans about the Apartheid era'. In *Journal of Psychology in Africa*, 19(3): 393–9.

Wits Historical papers: International Defence and Aid Fund (IDAF). Documents, reports, transcripts from Trial of 22, witness statements.

World Health Organisation (WHO). 2018. 'Gender disparities in mental health'. Available at: https://www.who.int/mental_health/media/en/242.pdf (Accessed May 2018).

Bibliography

Clark, N.L. & Worger, WH. 2016. *South Africa: The Rise and Fall of Apartheid.* London: Routledge.

Dawson, G. 2019. 'Storytelling in "post-conflict" times: Narrative, subjectivity and experience in community-based peacebuilding'. In S. Lehner & C. McGrattan (eds.), *The Promise of Peace in Northern Ireland.* Manchester: Manchester University Press.

Desai, A. 2012. *Reading Revolution: Shakespeare on Robben Island.* Pretoria: Unisa Press.

Dlamini, J. 2015. *Askari: A Story of Collaboration and Betrayal in the Anti-Apartheid Struggle.* Oxford: Oxford University Press.

Du Preez Bezdrob, A.M. 2004. *Winnie Mandela: A Life.* Cape Town: Penguin Random House (e-book).

First, R. 1965. *117 Days: An Account of Confinement and Interrogation under the South African 90-Day Detention Law.* London: Hachette.

Ghandhi, M.K. 1928. *Satyagraha in South Africa.* Madras: S Ganasan.

Gobodo-Madikizela, P. (ed.). 2016. *Breaking Intergenerational Cycles of Repetition: A Global Dialogue on Historical Trauma and Memory.* Germany: Barbara Budrich Publishers.

Gobodo-Madikizela, P. & Van der Merwe, C.N. (eds.). 2009. *Memory, Narrative and Forgiveness: Perspectives on the Unfinished Journeys of the Past.* Cambridge: Cambridge Scholars Publishing.

Kathrada, A. 2004. *Memoirs.* Johannesburg: Struik.

Madikizela-Mandela, W. 2014. *491 Days: Prisoner Number 1323/69.* Athens: Ohio University Press.

Mandela, N. 1994. *Long Walk to Freedom.* Philadelphia, PA: Little, Brown.

Mandela, W. 1985. *Part of My Soul Went with Him.* New York: WW Norton & Company.

Mbeki, G. 1992. *The Struggle for Liberation in South Africa.* Cape Town. David Philip.

Naidoo, Indres. 2012. *Island in Chains by Prisoner 885/63.* Johannesburg: Penguin Books South Africa.

Schadeberg, J. & Dyantyi, B. 1990. *Nelson Mandela and the Rise of the ANC.* Johannesburg: Jonathan Ball.

Sikhakhane, J. 1977. *A Window on Soweto (No. 25).* London: International Defence and Aid Fund.

Sisulu, E. 2003. *Walter and Albertina Sisulu: In Our Lifetime.* Cape Town: New Africa Books.

Index

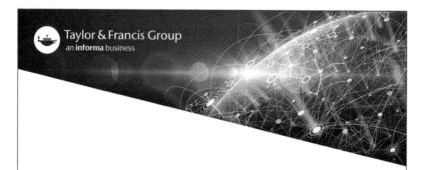